CIRCLE LINE

AROUND LONDON IN A SMALL BOAT

Steffan Meyric Hughes

summersdale

ABOUT THE AUTHOR

Steffan Meyric Hughes is a canoeist and sailor trapped in the body of a journalist. He has written for *The Observer*, *The Independent*, *Time Out* and various marine titles. He is currently news editor at the monthly yachting magazine *Classic Boat* and lives in Finsbury Park, north London. This is his first book.

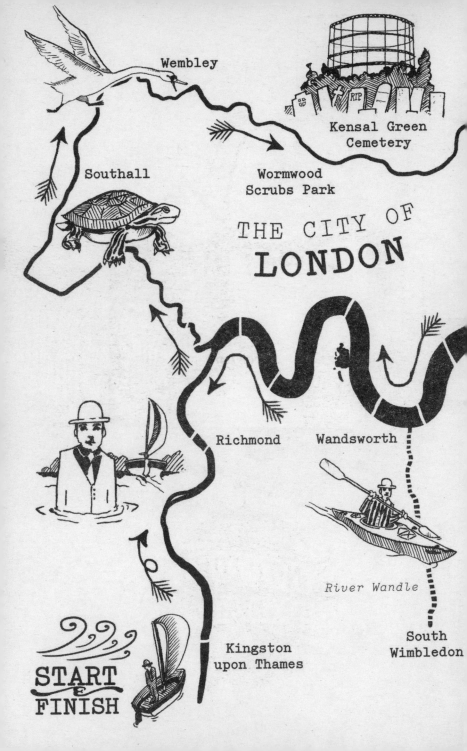

CONTENTS

CHAPTER 1
DAYS OF POWER, 1990

London: The train over the river, the 'power station wave' and a novel idea.

Every man must believe in something.
I believe I'll go canoeing.

H. D. THOREAU

It was only at low water, and better still a spring low, when the sun and moon combine to try to suck the water off the face of the earth, that you'd see the 'power station wave'. When the Thames ran out to sea leaving half the riverbed bare, you would see the cooling outlets of the Lots Road power station playing into its industrial little creek that resembled – well, to my mind anyway – a cataract of the White Nile. The power station, behind its façade of old London brick, hummed as it generated 92 megawatts of electricity rushing quietly through pythonous cables to power the tube trains running beneath the city.

Every time it was low tide, we'd get into our battered, blue, riveted-aluminium powerboat and skim west over the Thames from our canoeing club in Pimlico, our heads completely and magnificently filled with the fractured whine of the Tohatsu 40 hp two-stroker and the splashing of the hull on water. We'd arrive at the little creek in Chelsea, get into our plastic, dayglo kayaks, balance on the rim of the powerboat, snap neoprene spraydecks onto the edge of our cockpits and drop like seals into the river. Even from a distance, we'd hear the smooth, high-pitched whine of the Rolls-Royce turbines, like a fleet of muted 747s taking off, and the sound would fill me with a sick, nervy excitement I can still feel every time I'm at an airport – even at the most mundane moments of modern travel, like buying expensive post-9/11 toothpaste after losing mine at check-in.

On the cooling outlet wave, we would, over the space of a few years, learn the elemental craft of paddling a kayak on white water. As fifteen-year-old kids, it passed us by that some of the things we were learning were as old as civilisation. We were gear freaks, more interested in the next new paddle, new boat or new crash helmet, than in the reality of what we were doing. We should have guessed by the names. The Eskimo roll, clearly as old as the Eskimos who invented it; the ferry glide, crossing a stream with bows pointed upriver to compensate for the flow, sounds as though it may have been used by the ferryman of the River Styx. It took years for us to overcome our fear of drowning and just hang there upside down in the murk, before flipping upright again with a stroke of the paddle. Sometimes, after what felt like a near drowning on a cold February day, I would wonder why we did it. If we'd had more success with girls, no doubt we wouldn't have. Sometimes, on a sunny day, I'd cup a bit of the river in my hand and see tiny particles of warm brown river sediment floating in the water. I used to think the Thames was my river – I still do, even though I now know others have a greater claim.

If I wasn't on the river, I was by it. School was on the river, and I'd see it going to school, returning home from school, and out of the window I'd gaze at it all day long. Often I'd stop by Blackfriars Bridge on a fast spring tide and see the power of the brown water funnelling through the spans of the bridge, setting up trains of standing waves that bounced off the immovable, grey stone support stanchions in big dirty pressure cushions. Standing waves are just like waves at sea, but with one big difference: at sea, the water stays in the same place and the wave energy moves through it; on a river, the energy stays in the same place and the water moves through it. I couldn't look at a body of water without wanting to be on it or in it and, at nights, I'd dream of the river.

In 2002, Lots Road Power Station, like Battersea and the others before it, shut its turbines down and the wave fell flat. It was the last working example of London's cathedrals of power, the grand, brick buildings of the Edwardian era when inventors like Thomas Edison were kings and progress was the future. Lots Road was built in the early 1900s to convert the steam-driven underground trains to the new, cleaner power of electricity. It was the biggest power station in the world when it went up, and the first building in London to top the dome of St Paul's Cathedral. When it stopped generating, it seemed like the end of London's days of power and the beginning of its new incarnation as a centre for commerce and theme park commemorating its own past, a history of relics that were all the next big thing – and it seems unbelievable to me that a bunch of kids for a period of about five years were allowed to use the cooling outlet pipes of a power station as our playground, taking heavy-metal industrial technology for a joyride.

Twenty years later, I was commuting to work crossing the river on the Grosvenor Rail Bridge that carries trains into London's Victoria Station, vying daily with the free-paper hunter-gatherers for copies of the *Metro* and *London Lite*. It was 2009, and the news was full of austerity advice on how to survive the credit crunch – the word 'stay-cation' had entered the language. I'd found a job as a yachting journalist, travelling far and wide to sail other people's boats in all sorts of places and all in the name of research. And I'd strayed far from the river of my childhood, the one I saw fleetingly from a dirty window every day. The Thames looked blacker than ever that winter as the city lay under the heaviest snowfall for over a decade, which doesn't mean much in London, but the snow settled for long enough to cover the banks in whiteness and frame the black face of the river. The Meteorological Office was predicting 'a barbecue summer'.

This is a charming little *pas de deux* between forecasters and the public. Every year, the Meteorological Office lays its reputation on the line to cheer us up a little in the winter months by promising a record-breaking Mediterranean summer, and every year we choose to believe it. And I did believe it. Looking out of the train window every day as I crossed the river, then spending days gazing at the city in plan using Google Earth, I realised that, with the help of a two-century-old canal system and a small boat, it should be possible to sail and row around London, to float at less than walking pace through the magnitude of the city and view it from the perspective of its days of manufacture and commerce, to see how the old waterways had been deserted, becoming glimmering ribbons of solitude running through its brickwork like varicose veins cut off from the heart. As a stay-cation it would be the ultimate. You could only beat spending a week or more sailing around your own home town by walking around your own house.

I started counting the miles in spare moments. A loop starting on the Thames in deepest west London, east a bit on the Thames then onto the Grand Union Canal system for a semicircular clockwise loop around the western and northern reaches of the city, then back onto the river through the tidal, and seldom-used, Bow Creek, a quick loop east to take in the Thames Barrier, then all the way on the Thames back to the start point. London is hard to beat in early summer and I was keen to throw myself on its soft grass and drink it in. Seventy miles in ten days is not far. Even in my own imagination I couldn't use the word 'voyage' for such a tiny odyssey. But the Thames is one of the most historic waterways in the world and on her waters, as well as those of the River Brent, the River Lea and the Grand Union Canals, I'd transit, in that short distance, twenty-nine locks, 185 bridges, two tunnels, one of them a half-mile of darkness under the pavements of north London, two aqueducts and a tidal barrier. More than that, though, the city was my home, its waterways my playground. This was going to be an epic urban journey – and a trip down memory lane.

Getting hold of a boat was going to be the easy bit. And when a friend of mine suggested I could use the trip to raise money for the charity Sail 4 Cancer, which helps to send cancer patients and their families on sailing trips, I was happy to use my expedition for a good cause. And as a side-benefit, undertaking the trip for charity would open a lot of doors for me and ease my passage considerably: 'I'm doing this for charity, you know...'

The slightly harder bit was knowing where I'd pull the boat up and pitch my little tent at night. A small open boat offers no shelter for the night, so I'd be dependent on the kindness of strangers to make the trip work. I'd be entering a short period of genteel homelessness and throwing myself on the mercy of the softer parts of the city.

CHAPTER 2
OF DOWNSHIFTERS, KINGS AND SPEED FREAKS

In which the author waxes lyrical on the progress of man as seafarer and modern boatbuilder as downshifter.

If God had wanted plastic boats, he would have planted plastic trees.

ANONYMOUS

Man first took to boats before recorded history. If you count straddling a tree trunk and paddling it with your hands or by kicking your feet, then boats have existed presumably as long as man – or even ape. These evolved into the dugout canoe, which ultimately evolved into a fast and seaworthy craft, capable of coastal cruises and small forays offshore, and they're still built today in

17

much the same manner of taking a log, shaping the outside and scooping out the inside.

The idea of taking a tree trunk and chipping away every part unnecessary to the final form is an attractive one, a cross between boatbuilding and sculpture that ends up with a boat in one single piece. But it never took off in the same way that the alternative method did: to start with pieces and join them together. The first boats built in the modern way of wrapping a skin around a frame were probably the coracles and other similar craft, round bowls of just 4 ft diameter, built by stretching a cow hide over a willow frame. Men carried these from villages to the river on their backs and paddled with a single oar, weaving it in front of them in a figure-of-eight to draw the little bowl slowly through the water in search of fish. Boats soon travelled further afield: the Polynesian multihulls, slim catamarans and trimarans, fashioned of wood and bound with creeper, enabled their people to populate the Pacific.

Today, the kings are the 300,000-ton tankers and container ships, whose huge diesel engines revolve just eighty times a minute. The largest of these, since broken up on a beach in India, the *Seawise Giant*, could contain the volume of St Paul's Cathedral – six times. At more than a quarter of a mile long, she'd tower over the high buildings of Canary Wharf if she was planted on the ground, and if she were to sail on the Thames in central London, her bows would be under Chelsea Bridge while her stern quarters were still under Battersea Bridge – not that she'd fit under either: her control room would tower above the high blocks of flats on either side of the river and her hull would be aground on the river's bottom. Craft like these are the arteries that enable the products of globalisation to reach their markets – just as ships always have been – and to come across one making passage over the water, or to see one moored at night, is to see the pinnacle of man's grand and devilish ambition of infinite expansion.

Paddles and oars came first, then sails. Sailing has been with us for around 6,000 years. Considering its importance in discovering and populating the planet we live on, fishing its seas and establishing military dominance, progress was pretty sluggish for about 5,800 of those years. In the eighteenth century, clippers like the *Cutty Sark* finally achieved speeds better than the Roman triremes that were plied by oarsmen 2,000 years ago, and the tyranny of muscle was finally bettered by the harnessing of a much greater force. These extreme clippers, as they're known today, circled the globe on their trade routes at up to 18 knots, about 20 mph, but sailing speed only really took off after World War Two, when sail for the purpose of anything but pleasure was already dead in the water.

We can now, just, see the twentieth century as history, and in most areas it was a busy one: wooden ships and canons became nuclear submarines and intercontinental missiles; dreams of flight ended in a moon landing and whistling was overtaken by the iPod. And even speed under sail, that most ancient of practices, increased more after World War Two than it had in the six millennia before. In fact, sailing speed increased more during that time than the speed of cars. Today, kitesurfers and pilots of contraptions that look like giant spiders on skis streak over the water at over 60 mph, powered by nothing but the wind, and the record for any surface circumnavigation of the world belongs to a trimaran, in forty-five days, and it's falling all the time. It's a strange truth of the twenty-first century that the quickest way to go around the world without flying, is still sailing: the power record lags far behind.

In fact, speed under power has, like supersonic air travel, stagnated: the speed achieved by Donald Campbell in 1967, when he tore across Coniston Water to his death in a jet-propelled boat that looked like something out of *Thunderbirds*, is still near the benchmark. His peak speed of 328 mph just before he flipped and crashed to his death, was beaten a decade later by the equally intrepid Australian, Ken Warby, in a boat he built in his own shed, but not by much. One of my early memories was sitting in a little country pub in the Lake District with my parents. I might have been ten and I suppose it must have been near Coniston Water, where Campbell died. There was a picture of Campbell and the wrecked *Bluebird*. It must have been a newspaper report from the 1960s, framed. The memory is a vivid one because it was the first time I felt any interest in any paper with words printed on it that a grown-up had felt the urge to stick on a wall. No dull story of kings or queens here, no terse description of an undecipherable artwork or tortuous chronology of the people who owned the ground the pub stood on. No, this was real juice: speed, death – and a boat that looked like a jet fighter! Clearly, the world of adults had space to canonise men who lived their lives like boys, as well as the learned nonentities who were, to my mind, little better than glorified versions of the teachers at my school. I went to sleep that night in the old hotel, one of those houses with stairs that creak and run up and down in little flights and mazes, and dreamed of a world in which only feats on water were important and men like Campbell ruled the world.

My history on water, a lot simpler, started at the age of eight in a rubber dinghy called *Sea Dog* on a lake called Salagou in the south of France. I was on holiday with my parents and sister, and as they read on the beach in black tubular steel and cream cotton folding chairs, I'd blow up *Sea Dog* and lie in it savouring the simple joy of buoyancy, feeling the warm wind on my skin, then the warm water as it started to seep in through the seams, slowly starting to violate the walls of my little crucible of air, which is all you can say of any vessel. The lake was deep, its waters clean and blue and the red clay hills surrounding it made it look like a landscape from Mars. Every day, my mother and sister would lie in the sun, absorbing novel after novel, while my father would sit in the shade, slowly working through books about twentieth-century Europe with tiny print on pages as thin as loo paper.

It wasn't the most auspicious start to a life spent on water. A couple of years later, I learned to sail proper little dinghies – the roto-moulded pug-faced little Topper – on Kent's Bewl

Water, today a symbol of dropping water levels often seen on the news when there's talk of hosepipe bans. Later I'd paddle kayaks down furious torrents between jagged rocks in far-off places. But perhaps that was where the seed was sown, where the world of lakes, rivers and the sea started to marinate me in their inexorable, wonderful poison. Now I can hardly look at a waterway without a longing to float on its surface, dive below it – or even just dip my feet at the edge.

As I have said, getting hold of a boat was not the biggest problem, being in the lucky position of writing for an influential sailing magazine. Swallow Boats, a father-and-son outfit based in Wales, build a range of traditional designs in lightweight plywood and agreed to lend me the demonstrator of their Storm 15 dinghy, which would become home for the ten days of the trip. Father Nick used to be a farmer until his love of boats and boatbuilding proved to be too much. Son Matt wore a suit in London and knew about computers, and was paid to do so. Matt is now the driving force, and keeps a modern boatshed and a staff of a dozen paid men to build his boats. Say the term 'boatbuilder' to most people and they will imagine a craftsman of sorts, a journeyman who earns a decent wage and spends Friday nights in the pub. The modern builder of traditional boats is typically a 'downshifter' these days, although many of them hate the term, seeing the challenge and fulfilment more as an upshift. The greatest numbers are from IT, followed by a multitude of other white-collars in their mid-forties recovering from a prolonged bout of London – ex-journalists, ex-lawyers, ex-paper tigers of every hue. They fill adult education colleges in their scores, learning to fashion beautiful boats out of wood.

For the most part, they are passionate, eloquent sorts who escaped the rat race in London to go and live by water, the Hugh Fearnley-Whittingstalls of the sea. They are quietly ridiculed by some of the older generation of 'real' boatbuilders, the last men who were around to serve their apprenticeships in the 1960s and earlier, when boats always started with a tree. These older men are the master craftsmen, who love to gripe and moan about the youngsters snapping at their heels given half an audience. But they're also the ones who will give their all to pass on their knowledge to the ex-bankers and ex-lawyers... because they know, beneath their tough exteriors, that their boats will outlive all of them, and they have a genuine love of their craft that no simple generational rivalry will sully. Joseph Conrad, the ship captain writer, laureate of iron ships and grey seas, thought that the appeal of boats was attributable to their free spirits – allegorically at least, they belong to nobody.

Matt is unabashedly a modern boatbuilder, a young man running a very precarious business building sailing dinghies of Viking design origins to a build method that dates from World War Two, with rigs and other equipment that date from right about now. A dinghy built by Swallow Boats is a thoroughly postmodern mongrel.

This is the bit in every sailing story where the boat is described. Sailors sit more erectly and their beards generate a charge of static. Non-sailors slump in chairs, disappointed to have to skip pages so early on. As briefly as possible – the Storm 15 is a 15-ft gunter-rigged, unballasted, centreboard dinghy built in marine plywood with a self-setting jib on a club boom. The mainsail looks like an ordinary triangle, but the mast is in fact in two parts, the upper of which can be dropped at a moment's notice, useful for shooting bridges – that's what gunter-rigged means. The jib is the smaller triangular sail in front of the mast and the boom it's on, a length of wood running along its lower edge. This stiffening batten means that when tacking through the wind, when the sails flop over to the other side, the jib, stiffened by its boom, will flop over too. It's of a sort known as 'self-tending'. The boat only weighs 80 kg, remarkably light as a result of her plywood construction, lighter than real wood and lighter than plastic too. The boat is 'double-ended', or pointed at both ends (that's the Viking bit), although the phrase 'double-fronted' would be better, as it looks as though it has two bows – not two sterns.

It has no ballast – no lead attached under its keel or added weight inside – which makes it light and easily driven and makes me feel like I'm going to fall into the water or tip the boat over every time I step aboard. At its stern (the aft end), it can accommodate a small outboard engine, in this case a Honda 2.3 hp four-stroke air-cooled unit, mounted internally, the shaft going through a hole in the sole (the floor). The boat is painted the dark liquid green of seaweed and has a broad cream stripe running around the top edge.

Air-cooled engines are loud, as there is no cooling jacket of water surrounding them, and this one makes the petulant whine of a lawnmower. The Storm 15 also rows brilliantly; vital considering that I would be rowing or motoring all the way on the canals, their narrowness and low bridges and locks prohibiting even the lower half of the mast necessary for sailing. It is a lovely craft, pointed at both ends, as I have said, with a dipping curve to its side-profile (or a 'sheer' in the pretty language of marine architecture), and it carries all the added aesthetic joy of miniaturisation. A casual observer would know it at once as a design essentially coined by the Vikings, although its construction owes its origins to three inventions of World War Two: plywood, synthetic glue and the subsequent democratisation of sailing, once a sport for royalty and company owners only, men who'd race each other on the Solent, the little sea that separates England's south coast from the Isle of Wight, on huge yachts, wearing white caps and blue serge blazers with brass buttons, with large, paid crews to do the actual business of sailing.

King George V and the Kaiser fought closely as yachtsmen before fighting a naval arms race then a world war, and after that a series of men like Thomas Lipton and Woolworths owner W. L. Stephenson contested yachting's grandest trophy, the America's Cup, in 130-ft monoliths built for, in today's money, tens of millions of pounds. They never managed to wrest that trophy from America and today

Woolworths is no more – and it seems the only place you see Liptons tea is in clear glasses, milkless, kept in reserve by French cafe owners to sate English tourists who refuse to give up drinking tea in a country that doesn't understand it. We may have lost some of the romance of that era when yachtsmen spoke in clipped English and attended parties in starched white and dark blue, and the world map was coloured Empire pink – but today, sailing's for anyone who wants to try it.

A week before setting sail, I drove to the Newlands' boatyard in Cardigan Bay, on Wales's west coast, to pick up my little boat, and drove home the same day, arriving back on a warm summer's night at my little flat in Holloway. All the skittles were in place.

CHAPTER 3

SAIL WHEN YOU CAN

Surbiton to Brentford on the
River Thames: eight miles, nine
bridges, three locks and a series
of mishaps. Reflections on an
encounter with another voyager by
sail; the sanctuary of Brentford
and the slow train home.

*You can learn more about the human condition
in a voyage along the Thames than on any
long journey over the oceans of the world.*

PETER ACKROYD

There is magic in driving west across London on an early summer dawn with the sun just beginning to rise – particularly when the rest of the city is getting up for another day at work, but you have a little boat bobbing over the speed humps in the rear-view mirror. The streets were empty but filling, and commuters stopped to look at a little boat sailing down Pall Mall, Hyde Park Corner and

Knightsbridge as I trailed the little dinghy from my flat in Holloway in the hilly north towards the Thames Sailing Club just west of the city. In the western suburbs, window open, I could hear the London sound of the rising electric whine and clatter of tube trains coming up from their underground tunnels to run on elevated track over streets on little iron bridges. By the time we had reached Surbiton, the Surrey suburb of respectable England, the weather had broken and a warm drizzle fell with clouds of midges suspended within it. In common with many solo voyagers in boats, from eccentric Victorian sailors to now, I sometimes thought of my craft and me as 'we' when we were getting on well. At other moments in the journey, I fumed silently at the boat; these were 'I' moments.

I trailed the little dinghy by hand through the crunch of the gravel car park and launched it, leaving it lying quietly by the jetty of the Thames Sailing Club. It's Britain's oldest river-sailing club, with a bar full of appropriate mementoes – solid-silver cups, and black-and-white photos in the wood-lined club room showing lean, handsome men grinning in rows, wearing tank tops and holding trophies. It's an era I never knew, but one which lives on in the heart of my grandmother, an era when sport meant sport, not competition, and the greatest accolade for any English gentleman was to be thought of as a good sport. To make love meant to ingratiate, puddings (not desserts – heaven forbid) were always eaten with a fork as well as a spoon – at least by those who would be officers, enthusiasm was 'fashionable' and a gay little posy was a small, attractive bunch of flowers.

It was then, and here in Surbiton, that the gentleman dinghy sailor Linton Hope first hung over the side of a dinghy, holding onto knotted rope attached to the mast, to increase the vessel's righting moment, add more sail and go faster. Today, trapezes as they are now known, have become standard.

Perhaps competition, then as now, might have sacrificed some fraternity for the advancement of speed. These days, racing under sail on rivers is an anachronism, and only practised in the spirit of tradition. The boats just got too fast to be constrained by the width of a river like the Thames and today, dinghies built to plane across the surface of water need the wide open spaces of the sea – or are confined to waters of much less intrigue – reservoirs and gravel lakes.

My borrowed boat, an unnamed little 15-ft sailing dinghy, was loaded with enough camping gear for my strange trip. There was something rather sad about the camping kit. Even packed, it seemed to embody the meagreness of the shelter it afforded. It fitted into the boat wherever it could, and there was still far too much of it. Some of it had the tragic virtuosity of optimism: soap in an aluminium, army-issue soap tin, a razor blade destined to serve only as a talisman of civilisation and even a change of clothing or two. Other items, most notably the outboard motor and a large bottle of whisky, held illicit promise. They would prove to be more popular than the soap.

29

I stood for a while, the rain pattering down on my thin anorak, looking at the river. I remembered when I was younger and always on the river, I could tell what the tide was doing by tasting a drop of river water on my tongue. Such are the intimate pleasures afforded to those who travel in tiny craft, unknown to sailors of larger boats. At that moment, I felt apart from the river, contemplating a largely solo journey with no idea where I'd pitch my tent for most of the nine nights, and just the tiny boat and me set against the oppressive backdrop of a city of millions. It was an unease born of nothing more serious than the fear of failure though, and as I looked at the brown river I felt that unease dissipate: there is something relaxing about rain falling on water, the great hydrological cycle playing itself out in full view. Tiny bubbles rose slowly to the surface by the banks.

Terry, a photographer from the magazine I work for, arrived. In contrast to my thin anorak and T-shirt, he looked like a technological teddy bear, round and warm, lagged in a hide of fleece and red nylon and with huge zoom lenses hanging off each shoulder. 'I feel cold just looking at you,' he said. Next to arrive was my colleague from the magazine, Peter. With his wild grey hair, windowpane glasses and dry, surreal wit, he reminds me of a thinking man's Rolf Harris. He's also an authority on Arthur Ransome, author of *Swallows and Amazons*, and runs the trust which owns Ransome's old 1930s wooden sailing yacht *Nancy Blackett*, which became *Goblin* in *We Didn't Mean to Go to Sea*, a tale of misadventure in which four children on a yacht without adult supervision drift off their anchor off Suffolk and end up having to sail to Holland to find land.

It was good of him to have turned up, and doubtless more entertaining than another morning battling the inbox in our high-rise office in Croydon. Then came Ben, a Thames Club stalwart, a perfectly cylindrical barrel of muscle, body hair and enthusiasm who loves classic dinghies as much as his classic car (he hill-races a Sunbeam Tiger). It was Ben who'd arranged for me to use the club as a base.

I got into the boat and, somehow, rigged it. I'd never sailed it before, and never shot a bridge before, which is the knack of lowering sail to pass under an obstruction and raising it again after – all without stopping. This is the quintessential river sailor's trick, unknown to yachtsmen of the seven seas. And I hadn't sailed on a river, with its ever-changing wind angles, for nearly twenty years. Friends, drinking, university and, later, the glamorous pull of free sailing trips abroad with the job, as well as the insidious new stay-at-home pleasures like YouTube and Freeview, all got in the way.

'I think I ought to shake your hand,' said Peter, standing on the grey wood pontoon. I reached out, and nearly tipped the boat over. We shook. Ben and Pete untied me from the pontoon, a zephyr of wind caught the sail and I was off, 70 miles of London's waterways ahead of me. In my mind, I sailed east to the rising sun, a crowd of well-wishers, friends and family waving from the banks, perhaps even a press helicopter's rotors shredding the skies above my head.

I sailed 10 metres in a semicircle, the sail jammed on one side, and rammed the bank I'd just left. A red face from me and a chuckle from Peter and Ben, the send-off men... *this was definitely better than deleting emails at the office.* They pushed me back into the flow, and I headed downriver, straight into the path of an approaching pleasure cruiser. One of the most important and also most forgettable rules of sailing, like driving, is always to keep a visual account of what's coming up behind you.

I hardened sail and laid the best course I could, which means as directly into the wind as possible, to minimise the number of tacks I would have to make across the river. Now I was making progress in the right direction and picking up speed. The pleasure cruiser hooted its horn in disapproval as it motored by. A few passengers came to the rail to enjoy my embarrassment and admire the redness of my cheeks. Peter trotted along the bank, taking photos, but soon fell behind as the little dinghy picked up speed. There is no tide in this part of the Thames; the tidal reach begins a few miles downstream, at Teddington Lock, but I was already running late for my ebb tide, the six-hour flush-out that would take me from Teddington to my first night's stopover further downriver at Brentford Lock. This is where the Grand Union Canal system joins the tidal Thames, to emerge again 31 miles later at Limehouse Basin in east London.

Soon the boat was slipping easily through the water on a light, following wind. I shot the first bridge by messily dropping the top half of the mast and floating through, then raised the spaghetti of ropes and sail on the following side. It's a tricky manoeuvre, but one of the very few times I'd have to do it as any river bridges from here on would be too high to need it and any canal bridges would be too low to think of trying it. At last I was alone on the river, the rain falling gently around me, swans and geese in the grassy verges of the river's edge, a flotilla of kids in Optimists tacking nimbly back and forth, the smell of thunder in the air and then – in the distance – an otter's head popped up for a split second before it dived under the water. The green banks of Surbiton started to slip by as we headed towards London.

In 1969, three astronauts boarded the Saturn V rocket, an unlikely Jules Verne-ish marriage of complexity and crudeness and took off for outer space – their mission, the moon. Their craft may have been controlled by a supercomputer but its moving parts had to be lubricated by the oil of a monster of the deep, the square-headed sperm whale, whose oil was of a fineness that could not be synthesised in any laboratory.

At the same time, a thirty-year-old merchant naval officer called Robin Knox-Johnston was completing another navigational first in an old-fashioned wooden yacht, *Suhaili*, built of teak by men whose principal tool was the adze, the ancient boatbuilders' tool that looks something like an axe with its head turned through ninety degrees. She was built on a slipway in Bombay's docks and when finished was just 32 ft long. You might think that's quite long if you happen to look around and do a bit of spatial arithmetic that ends up with the boat sitting on your lap, its bowsprit pointing out of the sitting-room window and its mast rising up to brush the treetops on the street outside. But at sea where it belongs, 32 ft is tiny. A yacht of that size can be tossed end over end by a wave, or run down by a container ship without the ship's captain ever realising until he reaches port, with bits of yacht and rigging twisted around its carnivorous bows... some of the container ships putting into London's estuary ports of Tilbury and Felixstowe bear these marks.

One story, about a friend of a friend (although the friend swears it to be true) involves a sailor in a small yacht getting hit by an oil tanker in fog and being lifted neatly onto the bulbous section of the tanker's bow that protrudes just below water level. There he sat, in his little boat, skimming a foot or two above the water at 20 knots, until he pitched up at the next port of call. I reminded myself of these voyages sometimes, in fact every time I felt unnerved by the singularity of sailing around London in a dinghy.

Leaving in 1968 from Falmouth in Cornwall and returning to the same port 312 days later, Knox-Johnston became the first man to sail around the world solo and non-stop. For most of that time his malfunctioning radio meant that he was utterly alone, and in the throes of the most vicious seas in the world. The Southern Ocean, near the iceberg limit, is made up of the most southerly wastelands of the Atlantic, Indian and Pacific Oceans. Here, mountainous, freezing black waves are piled up by screaming winds, hurricane after hurricane chasing each other around the planet. Knox-Johnston was part of a race to become the first man to achieve a 'round alone non-stop' voyage, one of navigation's last prizes still to be claimed at the time. It's sailing's Everest – although far more challenging and dangerous and achieved by very few. Really, Everest is mountaineering's Southern Ocean.

Suhaili might have been a slug – but her skipper's extraordinary steadfastness and resolve meant that he claimed the prize. In his book, *A World of My Own*, he describes jumping into shark-infested waters to fix the hull of his boat, holding his breath and making repeated dives to fill a seam that had come adrift between two planks, all the while watching out for friends of the shark he'd just shot from on deck with a rifle.

Later, the boat is knocked flat on its side by the size of waves in the Southern Ocean and for night after night, he feels the keening wind but can't see the 70-ft waves coming up behind him, each one threatening to overwhelm his little craft and send it to the bottom of the sea. Sailing in conditions a fraction of this, even with a crew, is extraordinarily difficult. Forced to hold on for support with one, sometimes two hands, every simple task, from making tea to tying knots, becomes very tricky and long-winded. Seasickness can creep up on the hardiest and it's a struggle even to make enough food and to drink enough water to keep going.

Knox-Johnston was not just sailing around the world. He was sailing into unknown plains of the soul – solitude so intense, and for so long in such tight confinement and in such unkind conditions, had never before been undertaken – at least not voluntarily. Because of this the voyage excited the interest of a psychiatrist, who met Knox-Johnston before his trip and pronounced him 'distressingly normal'. When he returned nearly a year later, he had written himself into history and also sported a rather smart beard which he's kept to this day and which gives him a vague, unidentified sort of authority. I sometimes wonder if part of the attraction of a long solo voyage was the chance to grow that beard and spring it upon his friends and relatives without warning, and maybe scare children at family gatherings – but I've never dared to ask. Soon after he sailed back into Falmouth, the psychiatrist saw him again and made exactly the same prognosis.

If I'd entertained any thoughts of growing as a person while circumnavigating my home city, that momentous voyage was enough to give me pause. The London historian Peter Ackroyd once said that 'You can learn more about the human condition in a voyage along the Thames than on any long journey over the oceans of the world' but it's hard to imagine a trip better than solo around the world for learning about your own condition.

I met the legend – Knox-Johnston that is – at a lunch to celebrate forty years since his arrival back in England, just a few days before leaving on my own circumnavigation. After a curry lunch, we stood outside in the sun, smoking cigarillos and watching the shoppers, oblivious, pass by on the cobbled stones of St Katharine Docks in east London. *The Times*, who put up a prize of £5,000 for the first 'around the world non-stop and alone' four decades ago, hadn't bothered to turn up. We stood side by side for a photo – two circumnavigators – in front of *Suhaili*, which had also arrived for the occasion, and was sat on trestles on the dockside behind us. The preposterous idea of comparing our two voyages – one akin to something that might be undertaken by Stuart Little, the white cartoon mouse of the classic novel set in mid-twentieth-century New York with a penchant for crossing ponds in toy boats, the other a page from the history of endeavour – pleased me.

The rain was dying away as I headed towards my first major landmark: Teddington Weir and locks, where the upper Thames – the land of Victorian gents in straw boaters and stripy suits, the land of Jerome K. Jerome's famous Victorian comedy *Three Men in a Boat*, in which three middle-class loafers (not to mention a dog) become embroiled in a delightful series of little disasters involving mazes, frying pans and the dog – comes to an end. Much has changed since then, of course, but some things from Jerome's day are still the same: the pork pie will get trodden on, the lock will lead to embarrassment and the supplies will never fit in the boat. Such were my thoughts as I rummaged around for my squashed pork pie in my mountain of luggage as we headed towards our first lock.

Rowers skimmed past me as easily as water boatmen, those insects that skim on the surface of water. Their attendant launches followed behind, sometimes with a man shouting plummy exhortations through a megaphone. As someone who takes to the water to escape orders, one-upmanship and the rat race of the world on land, I found their flimsy craft and competitiveness hard to understand. Magic, to a sailor, is harnessing the wind – getting something for nothing – the surprise of a gust, the boon of a side wind, the trial of a headwind and, best of all, the moment when a change in direction means turning away from the head seas and wind and spray and running away from it in silence and warmth. To a canoeist, the magic is gravity, the free ride, and harnessing every minute nuance of current to go where you want. The surfer explodes forward at great speed on a moving mountain of monumental force, and the diver enjoys drifting in weightlessness. Rowing looks like a sport that cries out for flat, unanimated waters, like reservoirs and lakes – a sport that might best be practised in a swimming pool if only there were one big enough. My own rule is 'Sail when you can, motor when you can't and row when you must'.

I passed a floating shack, built up organically over the years out of an eccentric patchwork of blue plastic tarpaulin, corrugated iron and sections of plywood, and didn't know whether to categorise it as island or craft. Along the banks, the years were peeled back like strata of time. Big white-stuccoed Georgian riverside mansions sat by brick-built 1980s homes, playing fields, another disused power station and the towpaths that are older than the city. It was as though the river were cutting a canyon through history. Cormorants dived and posed, arms outstretched like scarecrows; flocks of Canada geese floated by in invisible locomotion, their paddling feet hidden from view, followed by flotillas of their tiny chicks, but my most constant companions were the little black coots with white heads and the moorhens, similar but with red heads. By now I was on an easy run, straight before a light wind with just the mainsail up, held loosely by its rope (a 'sheet' in nautical terminology) in my left hand, the tiller in my right, always ready to tack or change direction. At sea, the wind, and one's course, seldom change. On a river, even if the wind stays true to one heading, the meanders mean that you are changing your point of sail constantly.

At Teddington Lock and Weir, the non-tidal Thames gives way to the tidal Thames, alternatively known as the Port of London, the London River or, most dramatically, 'the tideway'. Here the Environment Agency relinquishes control of the river to the century-old Port of London Authority and little harbingers of doom started to appear around me. Little patches of floating rubbish washed downstream to swirl around above the locks. Later, a large, dead silvery carp, bloated and torn by unseen teeth from below, floated on the surface. Perhaps then, this is where London begins. At Teddington, the lock-keeper made his way towards me, filled with *joie de vivre* for the sun that had started to come out, the grass under his feet and the sight of a little dinghy filled with camping kit approaching, and he was quick to regale me with the tale of the lock's claim to fame as the set for the fish-slap dance in *Monty Python*. The popular opinion of lock-keepers has them as inflexible, irritable clock-watchers with a hatred of anything that dares float on their waters... a troll on the bridge for adults. The four I met during my trip were all friendly and helpful quite beyond the call of their duties. Imagine the generosity of spirit needed to conjure up a pleasant smile to accompany the fish-slap dance story – for the 400th time.

At Richmond, an hour's uneventful sail later, I dropped sail and, picking up a single oar and standing at the stern, paddled the boat into the second of the twenty-five locks I would encounter on the voyage, but not until after a passenger ferry had locked in to travel upstream, its dirty stern wave bubbling brown and frothy, the exhaust from its diesel mixing in like a warm, vaporous fart. I waved at the passengers lining the rails, and they gazed back, impassive and bovine.

The friendly lock-keeper (another one, see?) told me to grab hold of one of the chains that hang down the walls and, as I held on, the little Storm and I sank into a Victorian chasm of black, slimy brickwork. Little splashes of water fell on my face and arms and I wondered for a moment if the lock-keeper had produced a water pistol to take potshots at me with. A moment later the mystery was resolved: the lock wall harbours colonies of mussels, spitting the river out as the water leaves them temporarily high and dry when the lock is emptied.

Because I had been late leaving, my ebb tide to take me to Brentford, where I'd planned to stop overnight, was slowing down as it reached low water. The wind had gone haywire, alternately still then gusting lustily from all angles, and the little outboard motor refused to start. Rowing against the Thames would be impossible once the new flood tide started to gain pace and run from the North Sea back into town. Soon I was in a completely deserted stretch of river, with just the dark green vastness of Richmond Park, a woodland big enough to be home to herds of deer, slipping by behind the gently sloping banks, with trees growing over them down to the high-water line.

On a sunny day it would have been a beautiful place. Now it seemed bleak. I longed to swim ashore, walk to the nearest tube and go home, but the Storm 15 was now a noose around my neck, with nowhere to leave her that would be safe from vandals, thieves and the rising tide. After frantically trying the motor time and time again, I tried talking to it, softly at first, with whispers of encouragement and flattery, then by challenging it to defy me. I hissed at it furiously under my breath, then finally, in the strange relationship a man has with a motor (and this is a male thing, I think), I shouted at it with great passion and all the colourful encouragement I could muster, just as a middle-aged woman came into view walking a chocolate Labrador on the bank. Chocolate Labradors have slowly come into fashion in London's wealthier suburbs. I suppose they had to wait for the white ones and black ones to die. Long, agonizing moments later, she disappeared from view, and I decided to get the sail back up, even though the wind was blowing hot and cold, and I hadn't yet figured out how to reef it down to a manageable size.

There was a tangle at the top of the mast and, in desperation, I lifted the daggerboard – the retractable fin that protrudes through the bottom of the boat – and ran us onto the beach, jumped out, and pulled the mast down, bit by bit, to head height, where I untangled the ropes at the masthead, standing chest deep in the river while, all the time, the tide tried to sweep me off my feet. The boat, as if feeling its own power, tried to sail away from me as its sail unfurled and caught the wind. It almost made it, and I half-waded, half-swam after it as it sailed off, crawling in over the side and nearly capsizing in the process. In that moment, I'd nearly lost the boat, with what felt like everything I owned aboard it. For a few seconds, I'd felt as vulnerable and bare as a tramp. We forged ahead, sodden and over-pressed by the large mainsail at a great speed in gusty conditions, rolling worryingly from side to side every time the wind got behind us.

In anything more than a breeze a following wind is, contrary to intuition, the most challenging point of sail. Firstly, the wind can catch the sail and slam it over to the other side with great force in a move known as an 'accidental gybe' or a 'crash gybe'. The boom, the solid spar running along the sail's bottom, can break gear or knock the helmsman unconscious and sweep him overboard. Secondly, a boat sailing dead downwind will tend to turn to one side or the other, particularly when surfing down a wave. This is known as broaching, and was one of the dreads of the days of sail, when large schooners surfing uncontrollably down huge wave faces far from land could be turned on one side and then rolled over by the very wave they were running down. A ship in that predicament would sink with all hands. For me, a broach would mean getting my camera wet. Cautious sailors tend to tie the end of the boom to a strong point somewhere on the deck to prevent a crash gybe, or they tack downwind in a zigzag, much as they must when pointing upwind.

A few minutes later, the wind died altogether. Now there was nothing for it but Plan C, I thought as I remembered my own mantra – sail when you can, motor when you can't and row when you must. I rowed like a madman, breathing heavily to the sweep of the oars, surging through the water with a wake spreading out behind, but barely moving against the bank as the foul tide gathered force to sweep me back to my start point – and humiliation. I could hear a voice rhythmically hissing a desperate paeon of frustration and anger over and over… 'Got to get to Brentford, got to get to Brentford…' I was surprised to realise a moment later that the desperate tirade I could hear in my mind's ear was my own. Soon after that, I saw the sign I'd been longing for since leaving: Brentford Marina Floating Pontoon. I made a rope fast and collapsed onto the harsh platform of steel and bird shit, lying on my back, panting like a 100-m runner, before climbing the vertical iron rungs set into the wall, hauling my big orange waterproof bag up on a rope tied to my waist, a thin tail with a bulbous orange sting in its tip.

I sat down, sodden, in the middle of highly manicured parkland overlooked by flats. I found a whole French salami and wolfed it down in large, porky bites, washed down with some smoky Laphroaig, neat from the bottle. I like to think now that someone in one of those flats was gazing over the gardens, when a hissing, swearing madman suddenly appeared in an improbable boat, climbed up the wall dripping wet like a sodden tramp with a poisonous tail, and proceeded to consume a weird, booze-addled meal as soon as he hit the grass. But I'm also quite happy to think that my first day of folly was seen by no one.

It was a while before I had the strength to trudge off through Brentford Marina's blind alleys and locked gates to find Chris, who'd let me have the pontoon for the night. Chris, a gentle, bearded man of around fifty, had, like many who work by the river, a manner and form that seemed to have been gently eroded into shape by the implacable ebb and flow of the tide. He wasn't in the office, but engaged in his Sisyphean task of spraying goose shit off the wooden pontoons of the marina, a job he accepted calmly, as philosophical about his own boulder he must endlessly push up his hill as he is about the river. The tides run in and out, the birds pepper the land with shit from the sky and Chris is a cog spinning pragmatically in the cycle.

I'd thought of camping in a hidden spot of the gardens in front of the flats, but Chris advised against it. In my enthusiasm for the freedom of the city and for my own quest, I'd forgotten that people who live in modern citadels of tended lawns and security gates have an entrenched hatred of tents. And the kids who roam the towpaths of the canal, Chris warned, have an entrenched hatred of everyone.

Brentford Lock sits behind the white riverboats of the marina and flats, and joins the Thames to the River Brent for a few miles before the Brent becomes the Grand Union

Canal at the start of its 31-mile journey clockwise to Limehouse Basin, where it joins the Thames again in east London. I rowed the boat the last few metres into the River Brent, passing through the manned lock, and tied the boat up. With nowhere to camp, I was resigned at the first hurdle to having to catch the tube to spend the night at home. It seemed that the cries of the seagulls had taken on a mocking quality as I walked away from the marina back into the other world of Tescos and bus stops.

I found the station and, soaked through, took a seat among the commuters on the Metropolitan Line. Out of the window as we rushed, clattering, into central London, the sun was finally westering and beginning to turn orange at the end of a very long day. And despite the setbacks, the disappointment of running for home already, and the well-planned route remaining uncertain with pitfalls, I knew for the first time that going around London in a small boat would be possible. Probably.

CHAPTER 4

DEAD WATERS

Brentford Lock to the Piccadilly
Line bridge, on the River Brent and
Grand Union Canal, Bull's Bridge
Arm. Two miles, nine bridges and
two locks. The author rows under
motorways and through carpets of
fallen blossom in a world of his own
away from the bustle of the city.

*One generation abandons the enterprises
of another like stranded vessels.*

H. D. THOREAU

The next day I returned to Brentford at dawn and again
felt that thrill of dropping out of London life, through a
crack into an unknown world. The bright morning smelled
of summer, and music leaked out of the stereo of the one car
at the traffic lights as I crossed the road. A young white man
in a Rasta hat and long dreads wandered past the marina
entrance singing an ugly, improvised a cappella tune in a

keening falsetto of squashed vowels. 'Yeah, in ma youth Ah was foooolish. Now I've grown up and Ahm a man... ' Behind the marina and the river is where the canal starts its long loop clockwise to rejoin the river at Limehouse Basin in east London. It hardly ranks alongside Istanbul as a crossroads of the world, but it's still a surprising sight, with a working boatyard that was filled with ringing hammers and shouts the night before and was now quiet in the early morning light, surrounded by boats in dilapidated states and seagulls.

I made my way back to the lock I had passed through the day before and found lock-keeper Brian on duty, with a beard and flowing grey hair and the distinguished look of a man who has recovered from something, but I don't know what. He gave me a windlass, which is a large-handled key that you wind around and around in order to operate the unmanned locks – and they would all be unmanned until Limehouse. He gave me another one to take to Jeremy, his counterpart at Limehouse, where the lock is also manned.

Jeremy is a historian of the Thames and more so of the River Lea that flows into it in east London, and a few months ago, on a freezing night, I'd attended one of his talks at the Cruising Association, a yacht club of sorts with its headquarters at Limehouse. We sat, about one hundred of us, with glasses of wine and listened to Jeremy hold forth about the history of the River Lea, which in the nineteenth century was a place of such frenzied industry that seemingly half the modern world was invented on its rapidly industrialising banks: the urbane, slightly camp-sounding Martini-Henry rifle, the first breech-loader, the first modern gun in effect, manufactured in 1871; fulminate of mercury, then the most dangerously explosive substance created by man; and the electric light bulb in 1859, by a Mr Swain, although the glory went to Edison, who had the sense to patent it a full two decades later. In 1853, the substance perhaps still today the most symbolic of man's ability to synthesise all he beholds – plastic – was invented on the banks of that satanic little stream. The first plastics factory was established in Hackney in 1853 for the manufacture of xylonite. Considering its place in history, it's strange that the Lea is best known for a fishing manual. *The Compleat Angler*, set largely on its banks, was written by Izaak Walton and published in 1653, a mixture of instruction (like when to light your pipe), songs and verse. It's now revered as one of the great littoral bibles, and a quintessential ode to the English countryside. It has been in print for 350 years. In 2009, most of the Lea and its back rivers were closed off for their rejuvenation for the 2012 Olympics.

Leaving Brentford on the canal it was time to put away the mast. The next 31 miles would be rowed or, if headwinds made rowing difficult, made under power. I took the topmast and sail down, stowed it in one bundle under the foredeck, and removed the oars. I hold little affection for rowing, as you will have gathered, and not just because of its lack of subtlety and magic, but because I don't want to travel facing backwards, watching an unfolding view of where I've just been and never seeing where I'm going, which holds the excitement of the immediate future and is surely the elixir of travel. I never started the voyage with the idea of a challenge or any sort of physical accomplishment – but there is a disgrace in engines so close to every sailor's heart, that I could not face switching on the motor for the next few days – even if I could get it to start. There was also a toss-up here. Rowing, I'd be able to hear the sounds of the canal, but with the noisy air-cooled motor running, I'd only be able to see. For the time being, I decided to row. With the formalities dealt with and the boat ready, I tied up to the side of a disused narrowboat and climbed up into its decaying cockpit to have a better look at my surroundings. As bacon fried on my tiny meths stove, the mini Trangia beloved of super-lightweight backpackers, climbers and the Swedish Army, it was still just seven in the morning and completely silent.

The unmanned boatyard was still. An old Dutch steel barge, halfway through a refit, and two new steel narrowboats under build waited for the return of the boatbuilders. Next to the yard was an old wooden boatshed on the water with two narrowboats gently rotting away on the liquid blackness, while the sun began to warm the day. They're that rare thing: boats that, while still structurally sound, have been left so long that there seems little chance they'll be rescued. They sit in an aspic of neglect, untampered and layered with the patina of decades of stillness, their bright paint turned dull pastel from the sun and peeling off in intricate spiders' webs, hairlines cracking in geometric patterns. Over those grow real spiders' webs, and one day the boats will simply die of old age, shunted off to the side or perhaps half sunk, the bows forever pointing out of the black water, the unglamorous, unimportant wrecks of a shallow, disused siding of the canal.

There was something about the boatyard that belonged where the curlews cry, not in front of a patch of grass and a block of modern flats, and it's a wonderful, incongruous sight in London, which is becoming a place where every square foot of space is either home to old buildings or is being updated and worked so hard for its keep, that recent history and casual decay is never allowed to take root. Always, it seems now, the city must adhere to the fashionable orthodoxy of era-shock: the preserved and ancient and the gleaming and new, with everything that happened in-between scooped out and discarded. To the left of the boatyard there was a small island on a bend in the canal, housing what looked like two dilapidated clapperboard fishermen's houses. Brian the lock-keeper told me that the island, and presumably these buildings too, are home to an artists' colony – whatever that could be in 2009 in the suburb of Brentford. I watched it for clues for some time, but it was early and no one stirred.

I left, the oars creaking rhythmically in their crutches, drips falling away every time they left the water. For that first part of the morning, the light swirling a small boat makes while underway and the birds in the trees were the only sounds I could hear. Not a soul was in sight and at the same time, in the other world just a few hundred feet away from the canal, rush hour had already begun. Nearby, a Canada goose and her fleet of chicks bobbed along the surface of the water.

In London, and any other city with a well-developed canal network, you can't travel far without crossing a canal. Everyone has had a fleeting glimpse of a little idyll of pretty narrowboats, a strip of dark water, vegetation each side, seen in a second from a car travelling overhead or the window of a train. The more surprising thing is that, from below, moving at about 2 miles an hour in utter solitude, you notice the thundering arteries just a few feet above your head about as much as the car driver or train passenger notices you. That first day, I didn't realise I'd passed under a bridge that I'd driven over regularly for most of my adult life, until I checked my route later on Google Earth. Being there had felt less real than seeing a photo of the place shot from a satellite twenty Everests high. What I remember now is a bridge that made a hollow rumbling song, echoing through the quiet canal not loudly enough to drown out the thin bird sound. What I'd expected from the M4 passing above – the booming sound of metal heat-expansion joints as cars and lorries drove overhead, the collective Doppler roar of a city heading out west to Bristol, the west country and Wales, or heading back in – wasn't there, deadened by the peace of the canal, absorbed by the trees and the water that had been there for a hundred years or more, reflected upwards to the world above.

Brentford Gauging Locks, my first unmanned locks soon after that, were essentially beautifully engineered Victorian balance-beam locks sitting side by side. Unlike the others, these were operated by a series of large, square buttons set into an ugly metal plinth, a contraption that would have been more suited to opening doors on tube trains or selling condoms in pubs. I spent an hour running from button to sluice gate, sluice gate to boat and boat to button, stopping at each place in keen silence, waiting and listening to see if anything was happening, which was hard to determine. A lock is a combination of two forces: the gravity of water seeking its own level and human strength harnessed through gears and lever. To add a shiny electrical interface is to ruin this tactile exchange and, not being able to lean on gates and feel the water, it took me all that time to realise that the first lock didn't work. But the second did and soon after, I stepped from the concrete bank shakily into the rocking bottom boards of my little vessel. And we were off again, under oar, this time still on the River Brent, but also now on the Grand Union Canal, on Bull's Bridge Arm, to be precise. For the half-mile or so until the next lock, the two run as one: canal and canalised river, and a few joggers slowly overhauled me as I carried on.

I rowed under the solidly handsome arches of the bridge that takes the Piccadilly Line from Heathrow into London. Underneath a bridge is always a solemn, quiet place, and this one harbours colonies of bats in the summer months. Its form, high above the canal, threw a perfect shadow of itself onto a carpet of freshly fallen blossom that lay thick as a blanket, turning the surface of the water as solidly pink as a carpet. I rowed slowly through it, the slim bows barely moving the petals as our wake slipped through. The shadow of the bridge above distorted slowly into bulges as my wake moved through, then flew apart into pieces. When it reformed, it was invisible on the brown water, the reflecting pink having been washed aside. The shadow of history distorted by the progress of movement, I reflected for a moment, then nearly laughed aloud. There is something about solitude and movement that can make you take yourself too seriously. And I still had no idea where I'd sleep that night.

CHAPTER 5

STANDARD LIFE

Edinburgh: A diversion - the
author remembers why the waters
of the world mean so much to him,
while stuck on the ninth floor.

You don't have to be mad to work here – but it helps.

<small>ANONYMOUS</small>

*You don't have to be mad to work
here – you'll go mad.*

<small>ANONYMOUS</small>

My body soon went onto rowing autopilot as I became accustomed to my new habitat of hot May sunshine, parked narrowboats, green verges and the sort of overwhelming solitude that is so exaggerated in the midst of a city of millions. My mind wandered back to what I now think of as the 'lost' years. For about twelve years after leaving school, I left water's embrace and for a while it seemed as though boats and waterways were just a youthful phase I'd passed through. On reflection, that decade or more away from rivers and oceans is my single greatest regret.

Around the end of the last millennium, it was said that Standard Life was the biggest employer in Edinburgh, and I imagine a standard life was pretty much what you got when you worked there. I spent a year at a large bank, which was pretty comparable. 'You don't have to be mad to work here – but it helps!' was the cheery platitude bestowed by the lifers on any innocent soul who walked for the first time onto the ninth floor of the big satellite office in the south of the city. 'You don't have to be mad to work here – it'll drive you mad anyway' would have made a more realistic aphorism. Our job was inputting bank IOUs onto the new computer system. Reams of yellowing paper, each one signed by a person who had borrowed, or had wanted to borrow, money from the bank, together with the terms of repayment, had to be typed, one by one, onto digital forms and saved on our proprietary software system called something like Fortnox. They estimated it would take our team of twelve three years to do the job. In the end, it took a lot longer. We came to know the place, and each other, well, over the course of the six months I stayed there. We were like scuttling, hungry lizards in a huge vivarium divided by thin stud walls built of MDF with heavy, fire-check doors that threatened to bring them down every time they were opened or closed. Our team was made up largely of two camps: the 'someday people', who planned to do something better, some day, and 'lifers', who you could spot a mile off as they wore their magnetic door security tags around their necks to show they belonged, tags they would sometimes rub up against the electronic readers like affectionate dogs, when their hands were full and they needed to open a locked door.

I often wished I could look out of the window but the blinds were almost always shut on a sunny day, even if it was in the chill of February. For one thing, the glare bounced off the computer screens, making them impossible to read. Also, this was a building designed in the late 1960s with windows that don't open. It seemed to me a method of taking control away: if the offices were built without opening windows, its inhabitants were robbed of any choice in the question of their habitat, relying on the magic of air conditioning to survive. So the building was atmospherically sealed and the air conditioning only worked two days in five. I drew the blinds aside once and peeped out like a detective in an old movie and saw the famous mount called Arthur's Seat on the near horizon and then, one horizon further, the glittering line of the North Sea shore. I'd fallen into the awful postgraduate trap of so many – a pointless arts degree, an overcrowded job market and a city that lived, like so much of Britain, on the post-industrial prudence of insurance and investment and seemed to value little else.

Many of us were looking into the future in the same way a man might look down the barrel of a gun, and up there on the ninth floor, it was no exaggeration to say our hearts were dying. Seeing the sea like that had been a shock, and a reminder that I'd been away from water for far too long,

from the seas and lakes and rivers, the gutters of the world.
I think it was working in that office in 2000 that I realised
that the land was dead, or at least prosaic, and that only
water has anima, only water has a face that never makes the
same expression twice. In many ways, that year of purgatory
was a necessary low point, a smacking into the buffers that
could only mean reversing back out to try again, to live life
differently, to get back on the surface of water where I'd
spent most of my happier moments.

One day in the summer of 2000, the Y2K bug
disappointingly having failed to reset everything to zero and
give us all another chance, a man was mowing the lawn
outside the office. The smell of cut grass and two-stroke oil
was, I realised, the most bucolic thing I'd smelled for about
a year. I clicked onto Netscape Navigator and idly tapped
'Need to get out of here' into the search box. The following
popped up, although today, as I never printed it off at the
time, I paraphrase:

There was once a fisherman who lived in a small stone
cottage by the sea. His grandfather's grandfather had
been a fisherman, and so had his great-grandfather,
his grandfather and his father. The fisherman was
young and lived alone. The work was tiring, the
wages low. It was pleasant in the short summer, but
in the winter he sometimes thought he would die of
cold. Every morning before sunrise, come snow, sleet
or hail, he would walk down to his rowing boat on

the pebbles, his two oars over his shoulder, his nets dangling from the blades. And, every nightfall, he would walk back up the beach, his two oars over his shoulder, carrying his nets and the basket of fish he'd caught that day. On a fair day with a kind wind he'd sail for many miles. Over the years he'd seen basking sharks breaching from the waves. He'd seen gannets diving into the sea like missiles, rising laden with glittering silver in their beaks, skimming low over waves. He'd been close to God, that much he knew, when he saw a green flash over the horizon as the sun set. He'd seen God in the hypnotic glittering of silver wavelets stretching towards the far horizon. He'd caught in his nets creatures unknown to zoology. And just as surely, he'd never been as far as the next village down the coast. One day he returned from his fishing and unloaded his catch as he always did. Then he went to the inn for a glass of beer with his fellow fishermen as he always did. It was cold outside, loud rain falling on the windowpanes before snaking down. It was warm inside, though, with a fire crashing and hissing under the chimney breast. He told his friends what was on his mind: that he hadn't seen any of the land he lived on, and that he thought it was time he took to the roads to see what lay beyond. They laughed and asked him where he would go. He put his drink down, thought for a moment and replied: 'I'll take one of my oars over

*my shoulder and walk inland. I'll walk until someone
asks me what the oar is. Then I'll stop walking.' The
next morning, when he didn't show up at his boat,
the men went to his little stone cottage. Against the
wall was leaning a single oar.*

Later that day, 'management-level employees' (which was
all of us) went to training room A1 to learn how to answer
the phones in the approved, robotic manner. Far from
being insulted at the concept of being taught how to use
the phones, we were thrilled. Incoming phone work, as it's
called, was a soft touch compared to outgoing work, and
anything that broke the monotony of a day was good news.
Meridian Training Part One was going to be a ball! And
besides, the phones, big black machines called Meridians,
familiar to anyone who's ever earned under £17,500 a year
in an office environment, are complicated machines, riddled
with function buttons and connected to a central server by a
thick, colourful data cord that looks like a poisonous snake,
so that all calls can be recorded and monitored (for training
purposes).

Training Room A1 held a mixed-ability group that day
as it always did: the graduates hadn't read *War and Peace*
and the managers hadn't heard of it. 'Right – hello all!'
started Nicola, leading the session, brightly handing out
instruction sheets. 'I'll gie you a few minutes tae have a wee
read through them, and then we'll have a practice. I'm just
going tae pop out. Back in a minute.'

When Nicola came back in, we started an exercise that would seem surreal to anybody not grimly inured to the way corporate telecoms work at the bottom of the food chain. Each of us had to turn to the first page of the printouts, and receive a 'phone call' from Nicola. She'd pick up the phone's handset and impatiently tap out a random number, her manicured red nails clicking on the keyboard, then sit there, making a ringing noise, while using her other hand to appoint one of us to answer the phone. 'Good morning, Pontefract Life – this is Helen Browning speaking – how can I help you today?' 'Right, hold it there for a minute!' said Nicola, smiling at Helen, a pale young woman with black hair who wrote plays for Radio 4 that never got broadcast. 'Try saying it like this': she repeated the sentence in an up-and-down lilt – high on the first 'good', dipping down at 'morning', then hitting a plateau until 'how', then rising up, slowly at first then precipitously until 'help' came out somewhere near a soprano, dripping with joy, before nosediving sharply towards the end. I drew the rough shape of its tessitura on an x-y line on the back of an instruction booklet. It looked like the Alps. But it didn't take much imagination to interpolate a best-fit curve that made it look like waves at sea.

CHAPTER 6

SHIT CREEK

The Piccadilly Line bridge to just
above the Hanwell flight on the
Grand Union Canal, Bull's Bridge
Arm. Two miles, two bridges,
seven locks and one aqueduct. The
trials and glories of locks, the
sadness of modern technology, a
unique aqueduct, an encounter with
hoodies, R. D. Patcham, repairer
of small motors, and a stranding.

*'What's new?' is an interesting and broadening
question but one which, if pursued exclusively,
results only in an endless parade of trivia
and fashion, the silt of tomorrow.*

ROBERT M. PIRSIG

By the afternoon of that first day on the canal, I was
already at the Hanwell Flight. This series of six locks
is well known among narrowboaters who do the 'London

Ring', which is a shorter version of my circuit, from Brentford to Limehouse on the canals and back on the river. It's particularly dreaded by the wives of the retired couples who are the typical occupants of a narrowboat, for the reason that it's always these elderly women who have to do all the work, jumping on and off the boat and winding the heavy sluice gates up and down with the windlass before the back-breaking shuffle to push the heavy balance-beam gates open or shut. To give some idea of pace, the six locks raise the water level 53 ft in half a mile and it takes the best part of half a day to pass through.

Later on in the trip, in Camden, and in a bad temper after having navigated two locks single-handed, towing the boat through by hand with a bovine crowd just staring, offering neither help nor kinship, I made a remark to one of these men, calling his gallantry into question. I phrased it as a joke. It wasn't one. He stood at the tiller of their narrowboat with the self-important pose of a captain on the joystick of a 200,000-ton container ship docking at Felixstowe, in leather yachting shoes, the ones with the false laces that come out of the side, and, improbably, futuristic sunglasses that turned the entire upper half of his face into an oily, reflective visor. He told me that he had to steer the boat, as 'the wife' wasn't up to that delicate task. Well of course she wasn't, I thought to myself as I walked away. She's spent all the time she could have been practising that soft little job in the back-breaking work of winding the windlass and pushing the lock gates open and shut through the water of the canals.

As it turned out over the next week, I never tired of operating the locks. Everything about them seemed miraculous – miraculous that they still stood, two centuries old, and still worked as well as the day they were built. The forces of water, gravity and human strength stood still as the rest of the world changed out of all recognition in those 200 years, and the Victorian balance-beam lock still manipulates them as elegantly as anything else that has come since.

Going through locks, together with the need to keep to a timetable based around daylight hours, meant, physically at least, entering another era, one in which the lock, with its ability to make water 'flow uphill' was the technological marvel of its day. I rose with the sun, ate when hungry and came off the water in the late afternoons. Most days I didn't need to check the time to know when to stop for the night. The lowering sun told me.

The lock enabled the canal, but it was the expertise of young geniuses like Thomas Telford in levelling and bridging land for canals that soon afterwards enabled roads and railroads to eclipse them in the next era in transport, the steam age. This age, with machines that involved rapidly moving, concealed metal parts, brought with it the first machines of such complexity that they were beyond the comprehension of the lay user to understand in their entirety, just by seeing them at work. And when the railways did come, many of them were laid over or alongside the canals, on land that had already been levelled.

Today, that's the charm of canals, that they represent the last era whose props were understandable and serviceable in their entirety. It was the last chapter of 10,000 years, when man could finally catch or grow more food than he could eat, which gave him time to think about things... like how to build better boats. When these locks were built, the fastest man had ever travelled was on a horse – and the fastest he'd ever moved was falling off a cliff.

Locks might not have been any more than the sum of their parts but, as I was soon to discover that first day on the canal, they're one of those things, like see-saws, that are a lot more usable tackled by two. To operate a lock alone, and from a small boat, here's what you must do:

One: arrive and tie the boat loosely to the towpath. Tie the knot too tight, and you've wasted energy and time, as you'll have to untie it in a minute – tie it too loose and bad things happen.

Two: have a look at the lock. Is the water at the right level or not? On the Hanwell flight, I was climbing up away from the river into London's hills, so the right level was the one set by a boat that had just come down. As a boat had just gone up before me, every lock's water was at the wrong, higher, level. Also have a look at the date plaque on the lock gate: 1851. Read the more recent inscription below it, in marker pen: 'Eunice takes it up the arse'.

Three: walk to the near set of lock gates, realise you've forgotten the windlass, which is the key to the whole thing, return to the boat, retrieve it, walk back to the lock gates, and wind the sluices open to let the water start emptying out of the lock.

Four: hear the water begin to gush out from the higher level and admire the little torrent gushing away. Wonder how long it will be until the towpath is clear of dog walkers so you can pee behind some trees. Wonder if there will ever be a time at which tree cover and no dog walkers happen at the same time.

Five: realise that the knot, which you tied too loosely, is coming undone and the little fountain of water that is the lock emptying through the sluices in the wooden lock gate is sweeping your little boat back. Make a grab for the end of the rope, just as it disappears. Pace slowly back, waiting for the boat to come near the bank. Stalk it… wait… *and now!* Clumsily leap into the boat.

Six: grab the oars. Row back to the lock.

Seven: note that a slightly pissed-up crowd has just emerged from the pub to watch. There is a pub by every lock expressly so that this little theatre can have an audience of onlookers. The technical term for these people, who are as old as the canals themselves, is 'gongoozler'. A gongoozler is a person who enjoys watching the comings and goings of the canal. These ones were gonguzzlers. Or gonboozers. Tie up – firmly this time, ignoring the eyes boring into the back of your head with casual *Schadenfreude*. The water in the lock has now dropped to the same lower level that you are on below the lock.

Eight: put your back against one lock gate, and slowly swing it open. Now you've removed half of the bridge to the other side of the water so you can't cross without walking to the far gates, crossing there and walking back down on the other side.

Nine: realise you've left the windlass back where you started. Go back, walking all the way around. Retrieve windlass, then return (the long way again) to the gate on the other side.

Ten: walk that gate open too.

Eleven: walk back to the boat (the long way again). Start to untie the boat, only to realise the knot is now so tight you can't remove it. Look around to see no one's looking. Someone is! It's that lot from the pub – the gonboozers! The four-pints-at-lunchtime lot – sniggering! Hunch your body over the knot so they can't see and cut your own knot with a knife, an admission of failure as a seaman as bad as throwing up on the cross-Channel ferry.

Twelve: tow the boat into the lock, walking high above, on the edge of the lock. Once the boat is in, tie it up, close the lower gates, and basically repeat the whole process on the upper gates.

Fast forward to step **twenty-four:** pull the boat through the upper gates, and leave. Much though I resented the presence of the gongoozlers throughout my journey, I knew at the back of my mind that they at least had historical antecedents. A century or more ago, they might have been setting cocks at each other's throats or drinking themselves into stupors on ale, falling asleep in Hogarthian poses and laughing through gappy smiles. They represented a constant that lives in all of us – the desire to see folly enacted by another; whereas I, a sentimental Luddite voyaging the canals for pleasure, would not have existed. For all the irritation the gongoozlers caused me, they were a more authentic addition to the canalside than I was.

There was something very transparent and pleasingly immediate about the old-world simplicity of the locks. The workings of most things now bear little relation to their glittering hides. As Robert M. Pirsig complains in *Zen and the Art of Motorcycle Maintenance*, transparency of purpose has become so occluded that we might pick up a modern device and wonder what it does. It doesn't stop us wanting to have a more hands-on relationship with our lives, though: I remember rewinding music tapes with a biro when the battery life seemed in danger, and budging the stylus off a broken groove on the record. Others have fiddled with the jets on carburettors and blown pipe smoke through cylinder blocks. Now it's all impossible; everything is unmalleable and unserviceable; banging the TV will no longer make the fuzz go away, it'll just invalidate the manufacturer's warranty. The locks made me nostalgic for a simpler age: every part of them was necessary, every part obvious and visible and functional. After my initial stumbling comedies of unnecessary repetition, my best time on a lock was fourteen minutes. The average was about half an hour. Pirsig had his motorcycle. I, for the time being, had my locks.

Two locks into the Hanwell flight, I had a rare bit of company; a quiet man in his early forties and a boy of about twelve. The man had fine, enquiring features, but the boy was chubby and sloth-like. I guessed they were not father and son. They followed me for a couple of locks, the man doing his best to explain their workings to the boy, and after a few minutes the man asked me if I minded them gawping. I was pleased he had the decency to ask after the long moments under the oppressively casual gaze of the gongoozlers. We chatted away as I made my way very slowly up the flight. He used to live on the canals and he remembers them when they were a no-go area – full of trolleys, old bikes and drunks – canals straight out of an old made-for-TV murder drama. Irish, he said they were – the drunks, that is. He thought the canal was an underused resource. Judging by the happiness on the face of the boy as he took in the water, the wooden lock gates, the trees sucking in sun and radiating oxygen, I would say he was right. After a while, they left, and I was able to sit down under a tree to lunch – more salami on bread with olives and tomatoes.

I remember the Irish drunks from childhood. They were the bogeymen of the 1980s, wandering the streets in solitude, always with a bottle in one hand, a divorce and a firing from a job in the construction trade in their pasts. At least that was the legend of the Irish drunk. Soon after that, they were replaced by the black kids from the estates. Now the grizzly spectre of the urban landscape is the 'hoodie': teenagers with hooded sweatshirts, small, pinched faces and a peculiar manner of speech with a much-reduced vocabulary and, according to endless reports in the press that summer, quick to anger, frequently stabbing each other, often to death, over the slightest perceived insult. The canal seems to attract these kids in groups and, though I saw signs of some petty crime – vandalism and a drug deal – they left me to my own devices.

Near the end of the Hanwell Flight, a group of five of them were walking towards me from a distance and on the other bank, some dressed in what looked like a baby's growsuit but was in fact a complete hide of soft tracksuit. Their leader crossed a footbridge onto my side and approached. He was about sixteen, with the sort of white complexion that made him look as though he'd been buried underground for some years, and he called out a greeting: 'Wha' is you?' It clearly meant neither *who are you?* nor *how are you?* I guessed it meant something like 'Tell me something interesting about yourself...' I told him I was rowing and sailing around London and, after the obligatory 'I didn't know you could do that', he looked at me, looked at the boat and uttered a single word of approbation: '*Sick*.'

Instantly we had a shred of kinship. He was a fellow adventurer at heart, sapped by circumstance and peerage.

I tried to imagine him in the sun, with colour on his skin, and speaking in conventional English. Across the bank, the other four of his entourage were getting impatient. 'C'mon,' squealed one of the girls, and immediately my new friend's mood darkened and he shouted back in a false, cracking bass, 'Whassa matta wi' you – fuckin' crazy bitch!' Unperturbed, she simply repeated her plaintive plea – 'C'mon!' 'Aw raa, laters,' he shot at me and started to trudge back to the bridge, from where he'd double back to catch up with his group – but we were right by a closed lock. The gates of a lock have a handrail and footboard so you can cross from one side to the other, and I told the boy that he could cross here to save himself time. He stared at me as though it were a practical joke. 'Look,' I said, getting up and walking across. 'Is it safe?' he asked. 'Of course it is,' I replied – 'that's what they're for!' He shouted across to his group, 'Check this out!' Girl Two started... 'Are you fackin' insane?'

The boy made a loud tutting noise before giving up on the crossing, and shouted back his mantra: 'Whassa matta wi' you – fuckin' crazy bitch!' Then he gave me a timeless look that spoke the language of all men – *women*... He ran back to the footbridge and caught up with his group. They moved on. That they were fearful of crossing a 14-ft ditch of water on a very stout, broad walkway designed for that purpose confirmed a lot of what I suspected about the way modern kids are alienated from the physicality of the world we live in, from everything that makes the soul breathe that little bit more easily, and smothered by warnings about danger.

They had absorbed the ethos of safety handed down from above until it became their own; you can't, after all, control a nation without the willing participation of its subjects. Kids, it seems, are allowed very little risk or adventure in their lives these days, but you can't repress the desire of the young to stick their necks out and taste the winds of risk. Maybe that's why they form gangs and stab each other. One thing that has never changed over the last few centuries, though, is the healing power of the sea to cure this sort of malaise of the soul. On a boat, there is no choice but to co-operate and there are now so many schemes for troubled youngsters, who go under a series of pseudonyms like 'underprivileged youths' or, my favourite, 'deserving young adults', that boat owners are desperately in search of mildly troublesome teenagers to take to sea in order to get grants to keep their vessels afloat. I went on one of these jaunts, on a tall ship down the Irish coast, and it was heartening to see the kids climbing the masts, then inching out onto the yardarms, 80 ft above the deck.

One boy, who at the beginning of our four-day voyage was sullen, refusing to eat anything but mayonnaise straight from the jar, developed a selfless, rather heroic streak in just a couple of days, looking after a weaker crew mate and keeping everyone else plied with tea for the rest of our time aboard. It was the sea that cured his deranged diet by making him throw it up over the side – then the ship that cured him by letting him overcome his fear of climbing the mast, without even a safety harness to hold him close to the wood. As the skipper's mate asked me later 'why would you wear a safety harness? You're not going to let go, are you?'

My encounter with the hooded boy marked the last lock in the Hanwell Flight. Once above on the new, higher level, the canal high-sides around London's bowl most of the way, dropping back down into the bottom only as it reaches Limehouse in the east of the city. I only realised later, back on Google Earth, that straight after the Hanwell Flight, I'd rowed over an aqueduct that passes over the Great Western train line and under a road.

I returned to the aqueduct two years later, on a freezing day with cat ice lining the canal, bare trees lining its side, but still the joggers were out in their shrink-wrap of bright nylon, breathing clouds into the air as they went panting past, on the endless treadmill to losing weight and living forever. Windmill Bridge, as it's called, or Three Bridges, as it's also known, is easy to miss. A short steel square section carries the canal over the train tracks below, while a small road bridge passes just 10 ft overhead. Its maker was no less a figure than Isambard Kingdom Brunel, the nineteenth-century engineer who built much of the infrastructure of what we still think of as 'modern life' in Britain, and, to a point, kick-started the modern world.

He designed the first large, metal, propeller-driven ship, the SS *Great Britain*, launched in 1843. Today's equivalent is the titanic container ship or the 5,000-passenger cruise liner. The quarter-mile tunnel under the Thames connecting Rotherhithe to Wapping in the east of the city, started by Isambard's father in 1825 and opened the same year the *Great Britain* was launched, is the ancestor of projects like the Channel Tunnel today. Even this small aqueduct, one of his last, completed in 1859, crosses over another of his great firsts: the train tracks below belong to the Great Western Railway, connecting Wales and the west of England to north-west London, the world's first modern railway that terminates at Paddington Station – he built that too.

That same evening it was announced on the radio that the 330-mile High Speed Two line would be built, connecting London to Birmingham, Manchester and Leeds at 250 mph, a project that will be twenty-one years plus overrun in the making, about the same period it took Brunel to create the first 1,000 miles of his Great Western Railway with a band of men wielding pickaxes. Even this force of nature's plain little aqueduct is now a scheduled ancient monument. Brunel laid a skeleton of iron into England's landscape, and in my short trip around London, I would come across more than a few of its bones, many of them still in use, like the little aqueduct I stood on that freezing winter's day and the tunnel under the Thames, which now funnels the East London Line trains from one side of the city to the other.

In a gap between joggers, everything was quiet for a moment, save for the echoing flap of a pigeon taking flight under the road bridge above us and the constant trickle of water from the leaky lock gates, a tinkling that makes this part of the canal sound like an ornamental water feature. Someone had written on the side of the bridge *Our Government Kills.*

Ever since my moment in the Thames, knee-deep with the boat threatening to sail away without me, the motor had refused to work. It's a four-stroke single-cylinder and makes a high-pitched waspish buzz. Its air-cooling should make it reliable (one less thing to go wrong) as well as light. Much though I am entranced by engines – the suck, squeeze, bang, blow of the four-stroke is a magical continuum, and being able to use it so intuitively in a car is surely the most friendly relationship modern man has with something so mechanically complex – I understand little of their workings. I have not even developed a convincing charade to perform around the stage of an open bonnet. So when the motor refused to start again, I started asking around for a mechanic. You want to see R. D. Patcham under Putney Bridge, they told me. To this day, I have never met R. D. Patcham of under Putney

Bridge but, with ample time to do so, I invented him in my mind.

R. D. Patcham, aged sixty, remembers a time when he used to fix outboards all the time. Now he's been sidelined by the manufacturers, who make disposable engines with warranties that cover most of their serviceable lives and who carry out that servicing at faceless dealerships on the grotty concrete aprons that surround yacht marinas up and down the coast. His customers these days are skinflints who keep their old British Anzanis or Seagulls ticking over; simple, vintage motors from the days of British engine manufacture. He speaks in single syllables to young people (for whom he has no respect whatsoever), though chews the fat with his own peers, most of whom he refers to as 'young man'. He has a pencil behind one ear and lives in a different time zone – about twenty-five years ago, on the mists of my memory. R. D. (Dickie to his friends) remembers blowing pipe smoke through the cylinder block of an old Seagull, but his son, also called R. D. Patcham (Rich to his friends) never followed dad into the family business, or into his very mould for that matter. Instead, he does something inexplicable and dull with computers in the city. As far as Senior is concerned, it's daylight robbery.

I wished R. D. Patcham had been there to fix the engine now, because a minor calamity had just happened. The little Storm was such a joy to row, and I say this within the general context of how I feel about rowing, but in truth I was beginning to enjoy rowing just a tiny bit, feeling the surge through the water so precisely rewarding the efforts of my body... Anyway, the little Storm was such a joy to row that I put my back into it in earnest and soon after leaving the Hanwell Flight my left oar made a hideous ripping sound, a sound that spoke of many kinds of damage at once, tearing, splintering and snapping, and the rowlock (or, strictly speaking, the crutch), came free from the gunwale, showering its brass screws into the canal, a few falling into the boat and pinging around on the bottom boards. Thankfully, the rowlock fell inside the boat.

As I have said, sails were impossible because of the low bridges. Power was impossible without R. D. and the pencil behind his ear, and now rowing had just become impossible too. I had a closer look at the damage. The Newlands, who built and lent me the boat, wouldn't be pleased. And neither was I. I was up shit creek without an oar.

CHAPTER 7
FORCED TO CAMP

Marooned above the Hanwell
Flight. The author trespasses for
the night with a stray cat.

Our ship is magnificent; Albert has his
own landing stage at the garden, he enjoys
this sailing happiness very intensively.

ELSA EINSTEIN

In the grand scheme of things, this was not the greatest disaster ever to have befallen a voyager on water. The canal at this point is about 5 ft deep, and I was probably 15 ft from the bank. Worse things have, for instance, happened at sea. The real problem would be tying up to a bank somewhere and leaving the canal to find help – I was afraid the boat would be stolen.

It's an unwritten rule in travel that a place of refuge is never at hand when it's needed. The beautiful campsite you pass in the late afternoon will be the last one. The hotel with the one free room that you walk past because there will be others, better, will be the last room left in town. And the anchorage that you sail by after lunch, which looks ideal (but you wanted to go a little further before nightfall), will be the only decent one in the bay. And now it's dark and there's nowhere to stay the night.

So it was an immense stroke of luck that on my left was a peaceful armada of narrowboats and barges moored to a sloping, grassy embankment, locked off from the world outside by a chain-link fence, with a peeling wooden painted sign reminding the residents of this bucolic little place to make sure that the gate is locked at all times. By this time, a few children had appeared from nowhere on the other side of the canal. They were not there to help. The junior gongoozlers watched quietly, hoping that I would have to jump chest-deep into the canal to wade ashore. I stood up shakily in the bows of the boat and, taking an oar in both hands like a primitive gondolier, paddled slowly over to a colourful narrowboat, covered in an ornate Victorian serif, the words 'Riparian Joiner and Carpenter' down one side. I tied up and walked ashore. If only he really were a joiner and carpenter, I didn't care what 'riparian' meant. I was still of the assumption at that point that anyone who lived in a houseboat was either a freelance graphic designer, which might be another way of saying fashionably unemployed, a hash dealer or a fugitive from the Child Support Agency – and that the 'Say no to ID cards' stickers in some of the windows were merely enthusiastic dogma. Actually, I did meet a few watersiders who fell roughly into those categories – but the fear of ID cards was more real among a population with a significant proportion who live off the grid. One I met later in the trip had bought a clapped-out hull and dumped a small plastic yacht in it at a slight angle. He was a young man with an excitable, dishevelled appearance that gave him the constant air of stepping off a jetliner in the 1970s.

Now that I'd found a secure place to tie up, I was confronted with a second problem: it was too secure. The locked gate with the peeling sign might keep my boat safe – but the downside was that it kept me locked in by the canal. I paced up and down, seeing sheds, little patches of garden and boats, but I could find no way out and no sign of life. The day was drawing on and I decided to pitch camp, lugging the stuff from my boat, over the bows of the narrowboat and onto land, before finding a little spot under a tree out of the way at the end of the little embankment. I wrote an apologetic note about being a marooned mariner, stuck it onto the gate and went to sit in my tent, and had a lovely big slug of the Laphroaig, with a few drops of water, from a plastic camping mug that had been washed out with grass, staining all the tiny scratches in its surface with its chlorophyll. I set up the radio so its solar panel faced the last rays of the setting sun, and it spluttered into life. A silver tabby from one of the narrowboats came to join me, and together we listened to a chat show presenter moaning about the tube drivers going on strike for better pay, while the rest of the nation was in the grip of a pay freeze, families making cutbacks like holidaying at home.

For a long while, I watched a patch of grass two inches in front of my face as I used to as a child, and smelled the warm plastic, dead-insect smell of the tent. You begin to notice the life, the insects, only when you concentrate and lie still for a long period of time. This patience is the basis of nature observation. Doing nothing at all is seldom wasted time, if you are in a position to surrender yourself entirely to it. It's the only way you get to read the small print of life.

Later when it got dark, after sharing a supper of fried bacon, the cat and I practised more of nothingness. We gazed out for an hour over the stillness of the black water, knowing the immensity of the city pressed on around the next corner, then I crawled into the tent, the cat following me in for warmth, gripping things with its claws and pulling up clothing and bits of the sleeping bag as it shifted around, uncomfortable but not ready to surrender itself to its own devices. I tried to ignore it and tried to sleep, dreaming of old memories.

KwaZulu-Natal coast, South Africa, 2001. As soon as we were in the river, the driver pushed the throttle forward and the rigid inflatable, with two 250 hp outboards on the stern, reared its nose then flattened out, hunting over the wave tips. We passed under the ugly concrete road bridge from where the black South Africans were always dropping in lines for kingfish and other edible creatures of that coast, and the boat was moving so fast it seemed that only the intensity of the sun kept us pressed hard onto the surface of the Indian Ocean. Then we hit the surf zone, 6-ft rollers coming towards us. But we were faster, and played a game of cat and mouse, aiming for gaps, seeing waves that would swamp us and running tail for shore again. Eventually we made it out and, engines screaming, pointed at the horizon at about 70 knots, riding up and down the large, billowy swells of that wild stretch of coast where the Agulhas current runs southwards down the right-hand side of the African continent.

Winds come from and tides go to, goes the sailing school mnemonic. A southerly wind blows from the south: a southerly tide, or current, comes from the north. A southerly wind can, if it's strong enough, ruffle the surface of the southerly Agulhas to the extent that 90-ft waves are thrown up and passenger ships hoping for a free ride south on that great travelator of the sea, can and have been sunk without trace. The SS *Waratah*, a 500-ft-long passenger steamer of 16,000 tons, was lost on this coast in 1909, and no trace of her or the 211 souls on board have been found to this day, making her one of the most mysterious wrecks of all time. A local diver, Emlyn Brown, spent twenty-two years in a search for her but had to concede defeat in 2004.

The fractured wail of the outboards slowed down and died and we slopped around on the huge swell, rolling backwards, one by one, off the side tube, as dolphins arched in and out of the water around us. Almost as soon as we were under the surface, the ever-present sand tiger sharks swam over to take a look at us, as we dropped down through the water column to the bottom. The raggies, as they call them in South Africa, are thought to be harmless, but they look the part, with their snaggled teeth, and man-eater-sized bodies. They are often curious and come quite close. After a week diving the sites off Aliwal Shoal, I'd perhaps foolishly come to see them as friends and laughed as one came to say hello, serious and slow in his shyness, his sad face unable to reach out, unable to show any of the happiness of the dolphins flying along on the surface of the sea. It seemed the raggies were condemned by their ugliness to the status of freak show for holiday divers, always living in the 'middle ground' of the sea, as unbuoyed by the surface as they were uncomforted by the bottom. I wondered how they dealt with their endless homelessness and their cheap, lacklustre grey suits and I wondered where they slept at night. They seemed, with their dreadful teeth, peculiarly English, the travelling salesmen of the sea.

Another time, another boat. A year before the Boxing Day tsunami, a slow, wooden converted Thai fishing boat with brightly painted eyes at its bows chugged out of Phuket. As soon as we reached our target, we dropped over the side. The moment we looked down, the visibility was so good that all we could see was the wrecked car ferry. It was as though the seabed were made of steel and covered in rusty rivets. *King Cruiser* was always referred to as *Thai Tanic* by the invariably English dive guides who took us down deep to 34 m to swim inside its car bay. By that depth, I was awash with the bonhomie of nitrogen narcosis. Swimming with fish through the car hold, and up and down the companionways of a dead ship is strange enough. With the narcosis, it takes on the most incredibly vivid dreamlike quality. A large, colourful boxfish stared at me from a nest of rusty steel and rivets. Other fish, predatory in their obfuscation, crept back into man-made holes as we swam past.

The boat had gone down in 1997 with 350 on board after striking a reef. All hands were saved in fair weather and calm seas. At 87 m long it is one of the best-known wrecks in those seas, but soon, salt water will eat through its thin steel hull and it'll become too dangerous to dive. As we drifted out and upwards against the outside of the hull, a cliff face of metal, the narcosis seeped out of our blood and the surface of the sea grew lighter and lighter.

Later, I found myself half awake, and the cat had left the tent to return to its boat. It was dark and something above was brushing the nylon top of my tent. For a moment, I thought it was part of what I'd been thinking about, for the half-asleep state can melt dreams with reality and the tent seemed like a dome of half-thought and half-life, an extension of lethargic will. But it was a twig from the tree above. London, I mused dreamily, is alive with beauty and malice, individuality and homogeneity, bright Victorian sash windows glowing in a night diorama of dark green leaves and dark skies, and taxi engines idling in quiet streets. And tomorrow, this old canal would stop heading west away from the city on its trajectory to nowhere. I'd take a right turn, pass under a tiny bridge built 200 years ago, and start heading straight for the centre of the city, to my mind, a repository for everything else in the world. Briefly, I could almost feel what it was to live in the moment, to inhabit the now: an infinity of time, rain and motion lay behind me and an infinity of sea and future lay ahead.

CHAPTER 8

DRAGONS AND TRAFFIC CONES

```
Hanwell Flight to Willowtree Marina,
Grand Union Canal, Bull's Bridge and
  Paddington Arms. Four miles, ten
   bridges, two locks. A modern-day
 hermit boatbuilder who tells tales of
 giant terrapins living in the canals.
```

We may succeed in preserving the canals themselves
as strips of water, but we seem intent on destroying
everything that gave them interest and meaning.

TOM FOXTON

The next day I awoke fully and quickly to a perfect early-summer, eggshell-blue-sky morning, rested after a night under the sky. I left the tent and peed in the sharp morning air on some grass under the tree whose twig had stroked the tent in the night. From somewhere behind, I heard a voice

ask 'Do you want a coffee?' in a strange accent. Aussie? I
turned with a shock to see a short man with a bald head in
early middle age. He looked strong, despite his very pale,
hairless skin. 'Did you read my note?' I asked, realising that
I was a trespasser who'd yet to tell his tale and beg his bed.
'I'm sorry I had to crash like that, with no warning...' He
interrupted my awkward stream of apology, replying evenly
that he'd read the note. 'My question was: would you like
a coffee?' This was more like it. The kindness of strangers!
Random encounters on the banks of the water!

'I don't have much money,' he continued, 'but I have some
incredible Mexican coffee the owner of this place gave me
the other day.' 'This place' meant the narrowboat moorings.
Then the man walked around collecting twigs to light a
fire in his bush kettle to boil the water for the coffee. This
surprised me, as his narrowboat, the 40-ft 'Riparian Joiner
and Carpenter', looked homely. It transpired that he had gas
on his boat but couldn't afford to burn it. This was a man
living so hand to mouth that his version of life in the big city
was partly based on subsistence, burning the tiny amount of
firewood he could collect for cooking. He told me that he
was an out-of-work boatbuilder... *boatbuilder?* So that sign
was not just part of the traditional livery of his narrowboat.
He had painted it to advertise his trade. Here was someone
who could fix my boat.

We chatted for a while about wooden boats, and
boatbuilders. When he found out that I wrote for a sailing
magazine, he became wary. 'Don't you go writing about me,

journalist!' he warned. I told him I would have to write about him, as he was the most interesting person I'd met on my trip, but that I'd call him Frank, which made him smile. He seemed to like the name. Perhaps he agreed with me that it was as much a description as an alias of him. As we spoke, the kettle started to heat up over its fire of little twigs, and steam rose from its spout. The device, the Kelly kettle, is surprisingly simple and effective. A fire is lit on a small tray and the steel cylinder of water is placed on top. Soon enough, the good smell of fresh coffee was wafting up. When I asked Frank why I had to give him a false name he said darkly, 'They'll have the shirt off my back.' Whether he was on the run from the CSA or the taxman, or some other creditor, he didn't venture, and I didn't like to ask who it was who wanted his shirt. I found it unlikely that anyone keen for shirts would scour the yachting pages looking for them. Like many who dwell on the fringes of London's waterways, Frank lived completely off the radar. The land had rejected him, asked too many questions. The land had wanted money and answers. Here, on the water, Frank seemed completely content, a simple contentment that is hard to place or understand in the rat run that is London's own standard life in the twenty-first century. No rates, no taxes, no bills. He claimed nothing from the world and asked nothing from it, apart from the occasional bag of Mexican coffee.

Frank was waiting to heal from an injury sustained during his work as a carpenter before going back to work, but in the meanwhile he was enjoying working at his own pace on the renovation of his narrowboat. It seemed as though others, like the owner of the moorings who gave him coffee, were going to do their best to ensure that he did not starve, although Frank was at the point of queuing up for free curry and dhal at a local Indian Christian centre in Southall.

The canal in these parts – Southall and Ealing – is known by some as the Ganges, Frank said, for the floating coconuts and flimsy saris – 'awful if they wrap around your propeller'. This part of London is home to one of the largest populations of South Asians outside of the Indian subcontinent, a migration that started in the early 1950s, when the first settlers arrived on steamers at ports like Tilbury Landing Docks, east of London on the Thames. Today, the area is reckoned to be over fifty-five per cent Indian and Pakistani, and the railway platform signs are bilingual. A local restaurant accepts payment in rupees and there is a local radio station that pumps out the same diet of beat-heavy, sentimental R & B and hip hop as any other London station.

Frank was right about the coconuts; they floated in great numbers from here onwards for about 10 miles, bobbing low on the surface and barely keeping their heads above water in the wash of passing boats. The reason, I found out later, was that the canal here is sometimes used as an alternative site to the holy River Ganges for Hindu death rites. The coconuts are part of a post-cremation ritual marking a return to everyday life for the mourners. It seemed, in common with so much else in the immigration experience, like a brave, optimistic adaptation of circumstances to a new world; the Grand Union Canal is a sorry substitute for the epic Ganges.

There are dragons here too. The canal's inhabitants include red-eared terrapins bought in the early 1990s in the heat of the Teenage Mutant Ninja Turtle phase and kept by seemingly every teenage boy in London. I had a pair for a few years, which I gave to the boy across the road. Ten years later, they were still there, growing bigger and bigger in their glass aquarium. The boy across the road, of good heart, clearly believed in waiting for his friends to die, which they eventually did, after a couple of decades. The ones that were flushed down loos and otherwise disposed of now terrorise London's waterways, like the fabled crocodiles of New York's sewer system. As big as dinner plates, the exotic amphibians from the swamps of Louisiana and the southern states, with their beautiful stripes and red ears, eat their way through the native fish, newts, toad and frog spawn, and the odd baby bird.

According to a newspaper report in 2005, schoolchildren were reduced to tears at a north London pond, when they apparently saw ducklings being consumed by a group of ravenous terrapins. A mallard was later found with its legs bitten off. In another incident a park ranger at Hampstead Heath saw a duckling being dragged under water. The pretty little creatures that started life the size of a fifty pence piece had grown into smelly, often disease-carrying, antisocial beasts with a very sharp nip.

Britain is a nation that has somehow lost the simple knack of culling. It is a nation where one of the most hotly debated morality topics in recent decades has been fox hunting: is it OK to hunt them down on horseback with dogs in the traditional manner or not? The country men of blue blood who enjoy doing so clearly think so. They need culling, after all, they argue. And those who live in cities tend to think not, finding the sport barbaric, which of course it is. So now the cities are full of foxes, emptying rubbish, attacking pets and crying their hellish falsetto late into the London night. I'd often hear them nearby as I camped on the canalside. At first I thought it was a woman being murdered. At other times, they utter a double yelp that sounds like the remote central locking of a car being activated, one of London's late-night sounds that is usually drowned out by the hum of traffic during the day. Then the penny slowly dropped. The argument seems to embody two peculiar traits of the British character: sentimentality and violence. The voices suggesting a more practical system of culling, by rifle for instance, are few. It seems that if we cannot bathe in their blood, we are condemned to live with ever more foxes. So it is with the terrapins which, when caught, are sent to a secure holiday home in Tuscany, where they live out their days in a series of pools warmed by volcanic rock and Italian sunshine. Back here on the Ganges, they are sometimes seen on a sunny day, heads raised from the water. Confident and still, they watch and they wait. *The terrapins...*

We wandered to the edge of the Ganges, where Frank pulled a struggling frog to the safety of the grass. The vertical sides of the canal are a deathtrap for small animals, which jump in and drown, unable to leave the water again, he explains. A few feet away, a large shadow glides beneath the surface. It's a carp that Frank's been watching for weeks. 'The eastern Europeans net the carp, you know, and other fish like roach, and grill them up on those disposable barbeques you get in Tescos for a quid,' Frank said. I couldn't imagine a more grizzly feast than scaly fish pulled, thrashing desperately, from these murky rubbish-ridden waters and grilled on a little tinfoil picnic barbeque set. It was another comic tragedy of mislocation, migrants chasing the rivers and lakes of their fatherlands amid the traffic cones and shopping trolleys of the north-west London borders. The canalside anglers were after the same thing I was: wilderness in the canyons of a built-up metropolis, and our efforts sometimes bordered on the ridiculous. It was one of the many occasions throughout the journey that I wondered if living in England is a terrible sort of joke that has been played upon us. Perhaps that's why we are, to ourselves at least, so funny.

'It's the minks I really hate. They're strong little sods and when they're hungry they're brave as well,' Frank said with a shudder. 'They can attack otters and kill them, even though otters are a lot bigger. If they had wings they'd take over the world.' It seemed a powerful statement, as though Frank were connected by some mysterious cord to the birds and the beasts. How had he given the little sods wings?

Even in the imagination, it was a powerful leap. For most of the rest of the trip, I played mental consequences, mixing and matching the various creatures of the canalside, raiding evolution's parts catalogue to create terrifying demons capable of taking over the world.

The problem, a common one that often prevents vigorous flights of fancy in the English imagination, was the mildness of the landscape and its creatures, it's a landscape that created Larkin's odes to split-level shopping and caravan sites, while American writers were given odysseys across frozen plains, deep canyons and desert sand. And now, victim of a lesser struggle of the same kind, I was finding it impossible to forge demonic creatures from otters, coots and robin redbreasts. But my old headmaster grew the sharp bill of a toucan, gabbling nonsensically, scampering this way and that on his ostrich legs, snapping at boys' locks when they grew beyond the collar line. An ex-colleague grew an elephant's trunk so he could empty barrels of beer dry in pubs by sucking at the taps. A friend grew the mottled underbelly and flexible mouth of the greedy, fecund cod, and lay in wait for scraps of food, an opportunist looking for any chance to procreate or feed. For the next day or two, there were not many people I knew who did not sprout wings, tails and talons, and a few even developed compound eyes and powerful senses of smell. The visions ranged from the unspeakably sinister to the hilarious, and amused me for much of the rest of the trip.

Frank and I went to look at my ripped-out rowlocks. He recognised the Viking blood in the design of the little Storm 15 and pronounced it a proper little boat. 'You'll need it on the tideway,' he warned, referring to the Thames, added a story about the monstrous river swallowing a 70-ft narrowboat under Hammersmith Bridge, a story so unlikely it had the ring of the River Styx about it, and threw in some newer legends like the mythical 'undercurrents' that pull swimmers to their death on the Thames. Old wives' stuff inspired by the dark river. All the same, I thought about the pleasure boat *Marchioness* that sank in 1989 (more of which later), the many suicides, all the dead the great river had buried, the dank quality of its darkness, and the river took on, in my mind, some of the quality of a killer river, and this was the beginning of a slight, irrational doubt that started to nag in the back of my mind over the next few days as it drew closer.

I managed to force a twenty into Frank's hands for fixing the rowlock, a job he effected with Araldite and long, bronze screws. He also gave me a complete fix-it kit in case it happened again, but it never did. Frank was overjoyed, talking about the food he could buy and the work he could do to his floating home. And I was buoyed by the few hours I'd spent with Frank too. It's surprising how quickly loneliness can set in when you don't speak to a soul for more than a day or two, particularly in a strange environment like the place you call home.

'Good things happen to good people,' Frank called out with a farewell wave. And bad things, I reflected candidly, happen to all people. At that moment, a man came by with a wheelbarrow of riparian rubbish. Just why, or what he had in that barrow, and where he was going with it, I had no idea. But I didn't want to know why – it just seemed right that he should be there. It was like watching an Ealing comedy set on London's canal side. I'm not sure if Frank knew him either. But Frank, with a quality of timelessness about him, knew exactly how to act when a strange man comes along bearing a wheelbarrow full of rubbish. 'You going to throw out that old rope?' he asked, peering at the barrow's contents. 'You can have it if you like,' the wheelbarrow man replied, before continuing on his mysterious way. Now Frank was doubly happy. He had twenty pounds in his pocket and enough rope to make more fenders out of.

As I rowed away down the Ganges, I thought about another story Frank had told me. How, since his injury, he'd been stuck in 'this ditch', whereas before he'd lived on the Thames. He sounded like a sailor of old, wishing to return to the deep blue sea, asking only for 'a tall ship and a star to steer her by'. Clearly there is a pecking order here, of sea, then river, then, at the bottom by some margin, the canals. They will always be comical ribbons, forgotten by speed and progress. Perhaps there is nothing as funny as wanting to travel fast and failing, and nothing as lacking in intrigue as a waterway so shallow you could wade along its bottom, the water only reaching the height of your chest.

The buffoonery of the canal was underlined as I rowed away, gliding over a traffic cone resting on the bottom, brushing aside some of the coconuts Frank had warned me about, and spotting a large metal sign on the bankside. It had a line drawing of a man running away with a stolen carp under his arm, drawn in the British Road Safety school of rendering – 'stylised stick man', you might call it – and encircled in a red ring. 'Don't take fish from the river,' it said underneath, in English, then in Polish – then once again, in Russian.

Soon after that, a headwind sprang up and rowing into it became difficult as it caught one side of the boat then another and blew me into the north, suburban, bank. So I tended to overcorrect, but then I kept bumping into London. Rowing was hard under the best of conditions because of the narrow width of the canal here, and the need to face backwards meant a high degree of accuracy was needed, even with the centreboard up and the tiller lashed amidships, or in the middle. Do you sense a confession coming? As a last resort, I put more petrol into the recalcitrant little motor from the green plastic spare tank, then went through the motions. Tank lever down. Airscrew open. Throttle one third of a turn. Choke out. Safety cut-out deactivated. Pull on the string... it burred into life. For some reason, the motor needed at least a third of a tank to run. But it meant we were up and running again. Soon after that, I reached Bull's Bridge, a tiny stone bridge built in 1801, solid and rendered in white, with all the tiny curviness of a house from Tolkein.

On the right-hand side of the canal a marker pointed east: Paddington, 13.5 miles. Here, one turns right under the bridge, and the Grand Union Bull's Bridge Arm becomes the Grand Union Paddington Arm, and it's considered one of the dullest sections of British canal, a long straight run, or 'pound', in canal terminology, without locks and cordoned by little more than light industry and modern warehouses for most of its path. On one side of the canal were ranks of boxy, American-style houseboats, and for some reason I thought of the Mississippi River, a place I've never been: tough characters down in the cabins of the houseboats playing 'Texas hold'em' for money, sinking JDs and smoking cigars. Above, it's dark and the night is close. A streak of lightning splits the sky and in the distance a paddle steamer is making its way upriver... Back on the Grand Union, a huge grey, boxy building, only slightly forgiven by the bright sunlight, loomed at the edge of a drive-in trading estate. A childish script in bright colours on the side identified it as a Babies R Us.

Five minutes later, we approached another tiny bridge that looked as though it ought to cross a trout stream with children playing Poohsticks from it, but every few minutes an Intercity 125 thundered across on its way to Paddington

Station, vibrating the old stones and the air around us. On each of its steel frontage panels, a word was sprayed in large, white letters – THE. GAME. HAS. BEEN. LOST. An engineering team was busy pumping concrete into it to fortify it against this onslaught. If they stopped mid-pump, they explained, the concrete would set in the tubes, so now they'd started the job they had to finish it. As the man who detailed himself off from the group to explain this to me rejoined his mates, I could hear him saying 'All the way around London – in that!' The others looked over. One of them smiled and waved. I took the chance to fry the last of the bacon for breakfast, dipping the bread back into the fat, and drowning it all in chilli sauce. Soon after, the men started packing up their tools and I was off again.

I turned into a place called Willowtree Marina, one of the few places that looked just as flat as it had on Google Earth, functional and surrounded by a gridwork of new brick houses, each with a drive and new car outside. In fact, it looked as though it had been designed to be rendered by Google Earth in crude 3D blocks. I rowed to the pub, tied up and hopped out to a few bemused looks. Hemming in the pub and marina was a busy ring road with no pavement and no pedestrians in sight. Toy suburbia. Walking in environments like these that cling to the edges of cities means squeezing over and under barriers, crossing roundabouts, skirting gutters of busy roads and watching for nettles. I went for a wander and it was strangely enjoyable to feel concrete underfoot and to roam in a place whose artificiality matched that of the canal.

The pub in the marina looked like a mock-up of an airport pub from a film set. A mixed-ability crew had gathered by the time I returned and the place was lively with local residents of all ages, making the most of the only pub they had in this sterile zone. It was a happy place and everyone wanted to know about the traveller who'd arrived in a dinghy and tied his boat up outside the railings. 'You'll have to meet Adam,' the barmaid said. 'He knows about boats.' I get this a lot and it's often a blessing to be stereotyped in the company of strangers, as it gives people an instant handle on you, which is better than nothing. Meet Steffan – he knows about boats. Besides, boaty people always have a story to tell. She wandered out onto the waterfront with me and introduced us. He was sitting alone at a pub table/ bench set-up, patiently waiting for someone to talk to about boats, and I bought us a pint each.

We exchanged travel tales and it turned out we'd sailed in many of the same spots in the world: Portofino on the Ligurian coast, where the rich come to play in their multimillion pound antique wooden yachts; the Greek Islands where you can visit a new island every day, and where the last bus home is the inflatable back to your own yacht, anchored on the black sea, just like in the old Bacardi rum ad. Adam's story was a common one. He got divorced: the wife turned out to be a good housekeeper in the end, so she kept the house, leaving Adam living on a barge on a siding of a canal in suburban London. He seemed content, though, and we chatted for over an hour. By the time I left, three pints of cider later, I was pleasantly light-headed. And delighted that Adam hadn't, when he learned of my trip around London, asked the most unanswerable question: why?

CHAPTER 9

ANGRY SWANS AND SAILING OVER A-ROADS

Willowtree Marina to the A406
aqueduct; Grand Union Canal,
Paddington Arm: seven miles, twenty-
one bridges, one aqueduct and the
first men to sail around the world.

*Flying may not be all plain sailing, but
the fun of it is worth the price.*

AMELIA EARHART

On an autumn day in Seville, in 1522, eighteen men, led by their captain Sebastian d'Elcano, walked the streets in a ceremonial procession, watched by the incredulous townspeople. They couldn't believe that the men had sailed around the world because they didn't believe, until that point, that the world was not flat. Three years earlier, 237 men had left on five ships, and these eighteen, later joined by some stragglers who made it back from shipwreck and captivity on other boats of the fleet, were the only ones to return.

At the time, only a few educated men believed that the world was round, although in reality, since the beginning of recorded history, there was always the suspicion. There is a mythical, undated, tale of an Englishman who decided to see the world, and despite the warnings of family and friends, set off westward. After many years of crossing broad seas and encountering strange peoples he landed upon a shore where the natives spoke the English language. Continuing through this country he reached a locality where even his own dialect was used. Then he came upon a village that looked exactly like his own and where the people all knew him. Believing himself bewitched, he fled in terror, retracing his steps until he came safely home.

In 1986, at the age of eleven, I stood at the edge of Lac de Salagou, that warm place where I first bobbed around in a rubber dinghy, contemplating my own first circumnavigation. The lake might have been artificial, the valley flooded in 1968 to provide a stable head of water for irrigation and for forestry float planes to land on to take on water to tackle the frequent forest fires – but its depths have mystery. Monsters swim there, carp that grow up to 40 lbs that are patiently targeted by specialised carp fishermen, who hunt individual, known fish.

Below them are the lost villages of the flooded valley, not to mention a ghost hamlet that in those days lay half-immersed on the banks. Above it all flew windsurfers at great speed. The year before I'd swum halfway across the lake, to the slight concern of my parents. One moment I was swimming from the beach towards the island in the middle half a mile away, and the next – I was still going! This year my plan was to spend two days sailing around the lake's edge, with an armada of a dozen or so French children, each of us master of our own destiny in an Optimist dinghy, and the instructor, Jacques, who'd accompany us single-handing his Hobie Cat catamaran, a fast, twin-hulled sailing craft that reminded me of a water boatman, so easily would it skim over the water. Not so the little Optimists! These look like square boxes, 8 ft long with a stubby mast and an antique, sprit-rigged square sail. Designed for children, they are among the most popular dinghies of all time. In France they are referred to as 'Opties' and in England as 'Oppies' they are never given their full name by sailors. Their flat, wheelbarrow fronts might look slow, but the secret to their speed is in the flat hull that allows them to rise up and plane over the water at about 10 mph in the right wind. On a boat, and to a child, this feels like warp speed.

After a childhood spent reading the adventures of the Swallows and Amazons, finally we would get to discover our own Wild Cat Island, set up camp on the shore and eat around a campfire, in sight of the boats drawn up on the beach, on a warm night and under a full moon. Various

French parents arrived in Peugeots and Renaults and Citroëns, crunching off the thin black road onto the gravelly path to the sailing club at the water's edge and dropped off an assortment of children in different sizes and shapes, then drove off again. My parents stood chatting to Jacques for a while, then they were gone too.

Soon we were in our separate boats, rigging the sails on their little sprits and then we were away, sailing off on a perfect reach, a good breeze filling our sails from a right angle to our direction of travel, the fastest and most enjoyable point of sail. It may have been twenty-five years ago but I remember, with absolute clarity, holding the mainsheet, the rope that pulls the sail in and out, in my left hand, feeling and taming every nuance, every gust of wind, my right hand on the tiller, giving a little for every wavelet as I felt it press against the rudder of the boat below the water. When the harder gusts came, we leaned out over the opposite side of the boat to the sail, feeling the instant acceleration and the heeling of the dinghy. Moments before, the French kids had been quietly amiable, and I'd stood in their shadows, the only non-Francophone in the group. Now, not a word was said, no acknowledgement was made, but I knew that every one of us felt the same imperative: to win the race, get ahead, go faster. Unlike, say, cage fighting or desert marathon running, there is a limit to the exertion that you can expend in sailing. Once the sheet is trimmed perfectly, your brain starts screaming in desperation, trying futilely to send out waves of ESP to the boat. Go faster, go faster, GO FASTER! After a little while, the wind dropped and, leading the pack, I waggled the tiller furiously back and forth to maintain my lead, but soon lost it.

That evening we pulled up on a beach, and Jacques lit a big fire, around which we played games and I listened mute to children's voices as they swapped stories in French, a gentle burble of benign nonsense to my ears. I remember the smell of the fire, old wood from the vineyards that grow from the dry, stony land around there, and the smell of the pork chops roasting over its heat on a metal grid. The only sounds were wavelets lapping on the shingly shore, a warm breeze in the dark background of trees and childish laughter and voices, occasionally interrupted by Jacques' deep voice, filled with the rolling Rs and twangy vowels of Languedoc. Soon, paper plates were passed around, each bearing a fire-sizzled chop, a baked potato with charred skin spilt open and dripping with butter, bits of foil sticking to the outside, and a pile of lettuce with dressing squeezed from a bottle. It was one of the most delicious feasts I can remember. Afterwards, we spread out our sleeping bags and slept under a warm black sky. At one point in the night I woke up, and above, there were so many stars, still and shooting, dying and moving and glittering, that I couldn't go back to sleep for hours.

Since then, I've always needed to return to those sounds – waves on a shore, wind in the trees, food on a fire. They are the best sounds, sounds that we've known forever. The next day we sailed back to our waiting parents. Our first circumnavigation was over.

Progress had been good since the pub and by early afternoon the landscape had begun to change from deep suburban bucolic to a bleak inner suburban light-industrial wilderness of warehouses, bridges and inexplicable buildings. Suddenly, I heard a loud beating sound behind me, like the whumph of a helicopter blade punctuated at the end by a sharp percussive bang. I assumed the noise came from one of the many temporary-looking warehouses along the river. In contrast to the heavy industry I'd see later on the Thames, and the Victorian industrial relics that seem to cling everywhere to the water's edge, these newer, boxy buildings looked as though they were merely assembling electronic goods with vigour. I looked behind me and was surprised to see that the noise was coming from a swan. It was nesting season, and this was possibly a maternal, protective, swan. She skimmed across the water towards me, her keen, elongated neck like an arrow, trying mightily to take off and slapping the water as she flew towards me. I watched nervously, and grabbed an oar, holding it in one hand. The swan came to a rest, slowing down to a float, not a foot from the boat, glaring balefully at me out of the side of her head, mouth open. I rowed faster, trying to leave whatever unseen boundary marked the territory the bird clearly thought was hers. She came again, and this time I started to feel apprehensive. How many warnings would I get? Would I be able to fend her away with the oar, or would I have to break her slender neck? Swans, with their rococo curves, snobby demeanour and hissing character, have always been among my least favourite creatures, but the idea of having to swing an oar into one sickened me. Again, she rode alongside, this time hissing loudly, a spoilt little missy in an expensive white coat. Now I wasn't sure if it was play or threat. The third time she came, she stopped her run under my bows, and I could not help but run her over. She reappeared on the other side of the boat, disgruntled, but, thankfully, that was the end of it.

By the time that incident was over, I was approaching a long, thin, symmetrical concrete island in the near distance and then I was alongside it, rowing over the A406 – better known to Londoners as the North Circular, London's ugliest, most frustrating, traffic-choked artery. I hopped out and gazed over the high concrete wall. This wall renders canal boats invisible to the traffic below, so the miles of cars, glittering hot in the sun, had no idea that 20 ft above their heads, the wild little suburban operetta with the swan had just played itself out.

There was something perfectly desolate about the aqueduct. The water was rippling in the wind, the island seemed old, unrestored, dusty-looking and utterly intact. In contrast to decay or regeneration, it seemed unique, like a time warp. Although the air was totally still, I raised the sail on the little Storm 15 and rowed over the aqueduct, for the purposes of those stuck in cars below. A few motorists will have noticed a disembodied sail drifting over their heads that day. Until then, I doubt if they ever even noticed the nondescript bridge, let alone knew that in it was a waterway two centuries old.

CHAPTER 10

DREAMS OF LEAVING

A406 aqueduct to Paddington
Station; Grand Union Canal,
Paddington Arm. Six miles,
fifteen bridges. A call from the
mayor's office, an old wooden
boat and a lullaby for bedtime.

*I can't hear the shriek of a train
without wanting to be on it.*

PAUL THEROUX

It was soon obvious that I was approaching Paddington
Station. I'd been hearing the trains for miles as the little
Storm and I ran alongside the tracks laid soon after the canal
was dug. As I have said, railways are often drawn to colonise
the flatlands created for their slower predecessors: the track
was out of sight but I could hear it. Kensal Green gasometer
heaved into view as we rounded a corner, made beautiful by
its lack of detail, the angle of the sun transforming it into a

simple black skeletal outline, the familiar old-London form of the circular tower of iron.

Then we were running past Kensal Green Cemetery, the grounds of which are home to an astonishing 130 listed buildings, all various edifices to commemorate death. Near to me lay the bodies of the men who invented the modern world, including Isambard Kingdom Brunel, buried not too far from his railway and his Paddington Station – or, for that matter, his father Marc. There were more futurists of the Victorian age here: Charles Babbage, arguably the inventor of the computer when he devised his difference engine in the early nineteenth century. It wasn't built until 1991, to Babbage's drawings and to nineteenth-century engineering tolerance, yet it performed calculations to a greater accuracy than modern calculators: 31 figures after the decimal. Here also lie the bodies of the men who'd invented the first hydrogen fuel cell; the synthesis, or 'vulcanisation', of rubber; the transatlantic telegraphy cable; the father of production engineering and the first man to realise that heat was not in fact substance, but energy.

Around them lay thousands of other notable dead, a striking number of them naturalist explorers, astronomers, railway engineers and mathematicians – creatures of a century of exploration of everything, from science to the world itself. Present-day questions seem to be more about ourselves: where we came from, who we are, why we are, and how we can eradicate disease, get fit, get thin, get loved and live forever.

The hissing and banging grew louder as we neared Paddington Station, as the rake-snouted 125s and local trains pulled in from all over the west of England, Wales and the far reaches of the London suburbs.

I picked up my phone, which had started to ring in the bottom of the boat. It was a woman from the mayor's office. Could Boris Johnson join me for a day? This was not entirely out of the blue: at the lunch to celebrate forty years since Knox-Johnston's first solo non-stop voyage around the world, I had sat next to a busy man: the mayor's publicist Guto Harri, the one who appears on television every time Boris puts his foot in it. The mayor apparently was keen to publicise London's waterways, and I invited him to join me for a day on the boat for a photo shoot. My journey was, among other things, a fundraiser for the charity Sail 4 Cancer which, among other things, sends families with terminally ill cancer sufferers on wonderful sailing holidays, and the publicity provided by Boris would have been a great boost – and I thought it might be fun to have a VIP on board for the day, too.

Guto once described his own charge as possessing 'a rare combination of qualities. Man of the people and toff, classical scholar and buffoon, much-loved celebrity and politician.' I suspect Boris, when he'd expressed an interest in the trip, might have had man-of-the-people seasoned with a bit of buffoon in mind. I was more interested in the toff and the scholar, particularly the toff; toffs know how to row.

So the call might not have been out of the blue, but that hardly made it any less of a surprise. I arranged a provisional rendezvous with his aide and spent the next hour or two trying to imagine how it would happen. If it was going to be anything like meeting a minor royal, it would start with the King Charles spaniel sniffer dogs looking for bombs, and two mute, friendly-looking oafs in dark suits with concealed handguns. Maybe the man of the people didn't have that, though? The camera crew would be happy, with a straight, level towpath and a subject only a few feet away moving at walking speed. So Boris would be facing backwards and doing a bit of rowing, and I'd sit in the stern facing him and say something about London's waterways, like the Grand Union Canal. And it's a wrap! Except for one thing that slowly dawned on me: a little-appreciated quality of the double-ended hull form is that there is only one central seat for the rower. Behind that there are sideseats, making the boat balanced for three, but impossible for two. I would have had to sit on one side and the light Storm 15 is quite sensitive to crew weight – particularly when the crew weight is nearly 30 stone. We would look ridiculous, one of the mayor's oars chopping through thin air, the other catching deep, and the boat tilted sharply onto its ear, water lapping at the sides. It was quite conceivable that I could tip the Mayor of London into the Grand Union Canal and the footage would be played as the obligatory cheerful little item at the end of the TV news.

In the event, Boris did fall in, but not with me and not into the Grand Union Canal. Understandably, he had more important things to do than fool around in a small dinghy with an obscure marine journalist and couldn't make our rendezvous. Two days after I stepped off my circle line, he fell into the River Pool in south-east London, while joining in a day of volunteer litter picking.

The shadows were getting long and I moored up against a long strip of grassy gardens at the bottom of a steep embankment, 20 ft or so above the trains. Half a dozen narrowboats were moored to the bank but there was no one in sight. I wondered if the residents of the canal boats would let me pitch camp on their grass for the night. I hoped so, because it was the best spot I'd seen for a while, and if I went any further I'd be in the centre of the city, where demands on space grew ever tighter and the landscape ever more concrete and ever less conducive to tents and the quiet, undisturbed boiling of water for coffee.

There must have been a main road running by the station as over the banging of train carriages I could hear the gentler white noise of traffic roaring by underneath. This is one of the busiest transport junctions in London, but up there, raised just 20 ft or so on the embankment, it was a secret world.

London was all around and pressing closer, but I could see very little of it. I took a better look at the narrowboats, which were beginning to glow as the sun westered and darkened to red. One in particular stood out, with a cabin made by bolting the bodyshell of a Mark 1 Ford Transit van onto the hull. Behind me were a couple of winding pathways in gravel, leading up the bankside through mature trees, and I went to take a look. A perfect woodpile of logs drying for winter sat under a wooden shelter; little plots of red and purple geraniums and vegetables were growing and flowers stood in empty bottles.

Returning to the boat, I saw a woman in a long flowing dress and bare feet, playing on the grass bankside with two young children. Zoe, as she was called, had her own narrowboat, but it was away somewhere having its hull painted. I explained about the journey and she told me I could leave my boat tied up in her mooring, where it already was. But it wasn't up to her – it was up to someone called Steve, who was in charge of the moorings.

I made a two-second search for Steve by lifting my head and glancing around for a moment. Better to ask for forgiveness than permission, I figured. Zoe left and I removed the tent from its bag and threw it in the air, letting it fall to the ground pitched, throwing my gear inside then stepping away from it quickly. If Steve returned, I wanted him to see the tent first, then to meet me. Meeting me and the tent at once seemed too much somehow: *Here I am! And, as you see, I have already settled in...*

I wandered along the bank and heard the familiar sound of hammering. Two boats away from mine, and hidden under the boughs of a tree, was a beautiful old wooden river cruiser. It looked like a Herbert Woods design from the Norfolk Broads, 1930s, with its swooping, almost snobby elegance and deco curves. A floating holiday home from the days when a good night in involved an intemperate amount of dry sherry and a bloody racket coming from the gramophone. Still sounds like quite a good night in, come to think of it.

I stepped into the cockpit and knocked on the companionway door, partly because I was still worried enough about Steve returning to want him to see how friendly I'd become with his charges, and partly because I'm hard-wired by training to look at old boats. Like the teacher who is too severe with his children when he gets home, or the doctor who worries that his every sneeze indicates a rare form of cancer, I feel bound to enter the world of orbital sanders and cracked varnish every time I sense its presence. Also, I felt sure I'd identified the vessel's vintage and designer and wanted to show off my knowledge to someone who could corroborate it – and preferably be impressed by it. Working as a journalist in the very niche world of vintage boats, it is rare to have the chance to revel in the sort of solemn pride enjoyed weekly by the presenters of the *Antiques Roadshow*.

'Lovely boat,' I said when a voice beckoned me on board. You have to say that, by the way. Most boat owners are absurdly proud of their boats. The truth is not necessary, but thankfully neither is a huge amount of sincerity. A few nods and a few words, '… nice job you've done down here…' will do fine and you'll be back in the fresh air of the deck again before you know it. Ignore the fact that the boat looks beautiful above and dreadful below. Ignore the MDF table that was installed between the two bunks in the 1960s – yes, boats had all their original features ripped out then too, just like houses. Ignore the fake tongue-and-groove panelling that also looks rather dated but was in fact built in by the owner at huge effort last week. Ignore the fact that most of the rest might well look like the cafe bar of a Holiday Inn but with edges that don't meet properly in the corner. And, whatever you do, ignore the feeling that he is showing you this to highlight by contrast how good the boat looks above decks, as though to say, 'Just wait till I've done below decks too! Then imagine what the boat will look like!' Always assume that it has been done already and that you are looking at the 'after', not the 'before'.

There was no need for perfunctory insincerity here, though; through floating whorls of sawdust catching the low-angled sunlight, rolls of gaffer tape and electric power tools, this was a perfect slice of handbuilt thirties riverboat. I almost forgot my big moment: 'Is it a Broads cruiser – Herbert Woods – early thirties?' I asked as casually as possible and, just as casually, the man in the midst of the sawdust replied that it was. As if anyone in the world would know that. The man, who introduced himself as Dave, turned out not to be the owner, but a boatbuilder at work on his behalf, and he gave me a quick tour of the interior. Even for an old, handcrafted wooden boat, this was exceptional. Every bit of furniture was built by hand to match the curves of the hull, all Edwardian with a touch of deco (boat furniture has only ever given the slightest nod to the era in which it was built – the sea never changes, after all), solid to every corner – no plywood backs here – and in high quality timbers like old African mahogany and Burma teak. The switchgear was original bronze and Bakelite, and the lamps looked as though they were probably real Lalique or Tiffany.

The boat was that rare treasure – the Holy Grail all serious restorers look for: an abandoned time warp that's been left to moulder somewhere, rather than suffering decade after decade of 'improvements'. Billionaires hire scouts to search the world for years to find 100-ft vintage seagoing yachts by the old masters of yacht design like Fife and Herreshoff in this sort of condition for restorations that can cost £10 million or more. Of course, this is a rarefied, exotic game for the extremely rich, quite a few of whom are women, but the draw is that they end up with something that simply can't be built today. The slow-growth rainforest wood doesn't exist for it now, so much of it having been turned to less noble things, like television cabinets, or just burned down to create cattle-grazing ground to satisfy our endless hunger for meat.

We chatted for a while about our own restoration projects. Dave was boatless, and hoping to buy an old dinghy to do up and sail on the East Coast. Perhaps, like Frank, he felt bottled up on these little canals. I told him I needed somewhere to stay the night and he advised me to pitch camp and not worry about it. I already had, of course, and wandered slowly back to my tent. On my way there, I met an abrupt young American woman. I normally get on well with Americans because, unlike many English people, I don't dislike them and they can feel it, just like babies and animals can feel the presence of a friend. This one was as hard as one of the pecan nuts of her motherland. I felt I ought to mention the fact that I was camping in her back garden for the night, which she OK'd but I got the impression that perhaps it would have been better if I simply didn't exist. I sat outside the tent, poured a large whisky with the barest drop of water and shut my eyes. Birdsong, wind in the trees, the traffic, distant sirens and those trains, endlessly shunting and pulling in and out and banging. Over the top, the occasional muffled tearing of the sky by a jet bound for Heathrow.

Fifty yards away, Mitre Bridge stretched away over the canal, the roads and the railway. Its rust-pink metal was glowing, softening the angular industrial look of its late-Victorian engineering. This spot was, I knew, between Shepherd's Bush and Ladbroke Grove, not far from where I was brought up. We never knew, in decades of living here, that this place even existed so near above our heads. The graffiti opposite glowed silver as the dropping sun caught it, the brief blossoming of a garish flower of the city.

Further down the riverbank a trio of men sat, rods in the water. Their laughter drifted over the water and, when the traffic eventually died and I crawled into my sleeping bag and turned the little metal Maglight torch off, protected from the sounds of the world below by a 5-ft-high brick wall on the other side of the water, it was all I could hear – that and the occasional belch and scrunch of lager can. Every bed on earth has its own lullaby if you are interested in hearing it.

CHAPTER 11

ABOUT THE UMBRELLA

Paddington Station to Victoria Park;
Regent's Canal. Eight miles, fifty-
four bridges, two tunnels, seven
locks. Seas and rivers, the lives
of waves and a very long tunnel.

The world's true wildernesses lie under the sea.

H. D. THOREAU

I left early the next morning, head filled with Dave's dream, shared by so many living on the banks of the canal: to return to the sea – or at least the tidal river, the sea's finger – to feel the wind and the current, to see the skies that go on forever, to escape the mundanity of land and feel the endless energy of waves below and the cry of gulls above. The bankside was silent apart from the endless groan and clank of the trains underneath, and, at 5.45, the sun was already climbing.

ABOUT THE UMBRELLA

Later in the morning I was sailing. One of yacht sailing's many witticisms calls an umbrella one of the two most useless things you can have on a boat, the other being a stepladder. This is very strange, because a ladder could be extraordinarily useful for getting back on board after beaching the boat at low tide and going for a walk on the sand before the tide returns to refloat you. It must be a reference to the height of the mast, far beyond the reach of any stepladder, or the instability of the deck, which is always in slippery motion. The umbrella being so demoted is more understandable: it would never fit among all the rigging and spars and any rain will normally arrive horizontally before blowing the umbrella inside out.

On a small boat, though, an umbrella is one of the best things you can have, not so much for keeping the rain off, but for acting in its alternative role as parasol when moored, or for adding a bit of privacy to an otherwise empty shell or, best of all, for doing a spot of sailing when you can't raise the mast. In fact, without doubt the best sail I've ever had was courtesy of a large golf umbrella, and that was in the summer of '94.

In the summer of '94, I became one of thousands of English gap-year students who are placed in American summer camps, where Americans enrol their soft, video-games-addicted kids in the hope that they will become resourceful young adults and give the parents some free time to rent a house in the Hampshires or do whatever affluent American parents do. I became a canoeing instructor for the summer, though looking back on it, I think they might have hired the wrong guy. You see, America, and Canada even more so, are nations that were discovered and settled by canoe. Tough fur traders, gold prospectors and all manner of romantic-sounding frontier-era explorers and traders took a leaf out of the native Americans' book and built their canoes in the same manner, by wrapping birch bark and other skins around basket frames, loading them up and using the vast resource of lakes and rivers to traverse the country. Today, it's still a very popular thing to do. To put it as stereotypically as possible, 'Pop' loads the Old Town canoe on top of the station wagon, packs the trunk with a week's worth of peanut butter and jelly sandwiches, loads up the wife and kids, remembers to bring a flashlight or two and drives to one of the country's thousands of beautiful, wild and peaceful rivers – rivers whose little rapids send you gently on your way and where trout can be caught for supper in the evenings: like a family version of *Deliverance*, without anyone getting buggered at the point of a shotgun.

The canoe in question is a very light, open boat, pointed at both ends and propelled by a crew of two or three, who kneel or sit on thwarts, and stroke through the water with single-bladed paddles. Canoeing is as American as apple pie. Even Ronald and Nancy Reagan had a canoe called *Truluv*, though the allure of canoeing on North America's grand waterways was best described by the ex-Canadian Prime Minister, Pierre Elliot Trudeau, when he said, 'What sets a canoeing expedition apart is that it purifies you more rapidly and inescapably than any other travel. Travel a thousand miles on a train and you are a brute; pedal five hundred on a bicycle and you remain basically a bourgeois; paddle a hundred in a canoe and you are already a child of nature.' I could not have phrased it better.

However, canoeing has nothing to do with what I did, which was paddling short, stubby, plastic boats, into which you are sealed as you sit on the bottom, legs extended in front, body emerging through a small cockpit to form a half-man half-boat hybrid. When the British Victorian explorer, 'Rob Roy' MacGregor, explored the waterways in such a craft in the late nineteenth century, natives in Jordan thought him a river-borne minotaur – half-boat, half-man – and attacked him in fear. There is no canoeing history in Britain and very few canoes. What we do in Britain is, technically, called kayaking, a distinction North Americans, with a rich history in both, take seriously. In Britain, we just called them all canoes, preferring to do away with the ugly palindrome 'kayak'. I knew nothing about canoes.

It turned out not to be too much of a problem; after a few hours on the camp 'pond' with an American camp counsellor, I'd managed to nail the elusive 'J stroke', the forward-motion stroke that enables a solo canoeist to keep going in a straight line without swapping the paddle from side to side – a habit as ugly as it is inefficient.

The next week, I left in one of the camp's minibuses with two other counsellors and four kids to spend four days on the river.

We paddled down little riffling rapids and got stuck in large swathes of reeds that reminded me of the scene in *The African Queen* where the little river steamer gets lost in these forests for hours. We saw bald eagles and once, from our campsite on a misty morning, a moose wandered into our little ring of tents and moved around slowly in absolute silence for a few seconds before suddenly cantering off when he heard us all whispering '*Ssshhhh – a moose!*' We didn't see a living soul for four days. At night, when the kids had gone to bed, the two counsellors and I smoked, drank beer and told stories of ghosts and murders in the still night air. Or rather, the other two told ghost stories. I hadn't packed any for my trip to America, assuming the done thing was the same as in Britain, which is to tell lies and crack obscene jokes.

On the fourth day, the river emptied into a lake. After the magic of going with the flow, the static water of a lake feels like paddling through treacle, but the camp counsellors, old hands at this, had brought an umbrella and, the wind behind us, we opened it up and stood in the bows holding it out to the wind along with anything else we could fly. Propelled by a messy jury rig of umbrellas, rucksacks and anoraks, we moved forward. What this lacked in sophistication, it made up for in immediacy: standing up in the bows of our respective canoes, which we rafted together for stability, we were the masts, the standing rigging and the boom, our bodies the conduit for the gentle and immense power of the wind. A little wave gurgled at the bows and we surged before the wind for miles before reaching the shore that was our exit for the trip.

Later, I led a group of four of the kids on a seven-day special, hiking a 100-mile section of the Appalachian Trail, the longest walkers' trail in the world at nearly 2,200 miles. Walking up and down steep hills with heavy backpacks was torture. This was quite a hearty camp, and I was supposed to be grateful I'd been invited to lead this trip with four of the older boys, all of whom were considerably larger, stronger and fitter than me. It was a kind gesture to a guest in their nation and, of course, there were wonderful moments – cresting hills and seeing views of hills and forests that went for miles, dotted with pools of reflective silver marking the lakes, and the shining silver ribbons of rivers that connected them. But it was back-breakingly hard slog, and it was down there on those streams draining the hills where I wanted to be.

Away from the silver ribbons and lakes of Maine and back on the brown, rubbish-filled ditch in north London, I was at it again, umbrella out and a slight following wind sending us on our way. It was harder this time, as, with no one to steer, I had to stand awkwardly in the middle of the boat, one hand holding the umbrella and the other manning the tiller. I kept it up for as long as I could, then settled back to the oars, then got fed up with that too. After a while, I started up the motor, which made its petulant lawnmower whine echo off the buildings on either side of us. The two most useless things on a boat are not a stepladder and an umbrella. They are champagne flutes and AA membership.

I remember once shipping aboard a 24-ton wooden sailing pilot cutter in a Fastnet Race. The Fastnet is a venerable old ocean race for yachts that leaves from the Isle of Wight, sails west, rounds the Fastnet Rock off the southern tip of Ireland and returns to Plymouth, a distance of 605 miles as the crow flies. This particular trip, undertaken with a scratch crew of enthusiasts chartering their berths, was for the magazine: 'Do the Fastnet on a traditional wooden boat and write it up.' After four days or so, we were racing through a Celtic Sea dusk, a hundred miles off Land's End. A day of good wind had heaped the sea up into smooth, uniform waves, 10 ft or 15 ft high, breaking a little, their tips blowing away softly before us. We were running with wind and waves, all sail pulling, everything in perfect balance and under powerful, quiet load. I was on the left side of the cockpit, looking up to see our riding light, the colour of ruby port as they must be according to the laws of the sea, throwing its glow onto the white sail. Down at deck level, the side of the boat was riding just an inch above the black sea and occasionally a wave would wash aboard and sweep down the side deck bow to stern, glittering in shades of green and yellow.

I'd seen phosphorescence before, sailing around the Greek and Turkish islands. We were cruising on a 54-ft pre-war wooden ketch that time, and would drop anchor outside a different island each night and go ashore in the rigid inflatable. Every night my girlfriend and I, two of our friends, the eccentric lady owner of the boat, and the two Turkish crewmen, would eat grilled octopus, thick and salty, and Greek salad with feta and olives, and drink a bit too much raki or retsina under the stars. In night's darkness we'd return to the boat, its silhouette just visible a few hundred yards away from the old stone quayside, in utter silence apart from the Turkish crew chatting at the helm and the plaintive whine of two-stroke power as we headed back to the boat on our little inflatable dinghy. And some nights, our wake would stretch out behind us glittering like underwater sparklers.

But to see phosphorescence on that cold summer's night in the Celtic Sea was to feel a benevolent life force slopping onto the boat. The waves marched away to the horizon in front of us endlessly. As each one approached the stern we'd lift up and surf away before it, borne on its power. A firm handle on the tiller was needed to counteract the tendency to turn side-on to the wave. Using a wooden tiller to steer a heavy wooden boat through this sort of sea was to feel a connection with great force and it was then that I first started to put into words what it is about the sea that captivates those who sail upon it: the sea is an ever-changing canvas painted by unimaginable powers: the wind, the sky and the rotation of the planet itself.

The American Henry David Thoreau, the famously peevish, judgemental and smugly wholesome mid-nineteenth-century New England moralist and environmentalist, who wrote the 1854 classic *Walden* about his time spent living the life of a semi-hermit in the New England woods, once wrote that 'The land is vulgar; but the sea is subtle.' Thoreau, for all his faults and ornately masculine prose, was never afraid to speak plainly and had a way of explaining better than anyone else man's connection with his environment and with his inner tyrant – the tyrant that demanded material wealth, objects and timetables. On newspapers, he was sure that 'If you read a story once, you've read it every time. There is a lot of repetition, which places news in the category of gossip. They who edit and read it are old women over their tea.' On materialism: 'I think that the man is at a dead set who has got through a knot hole or a gateway where his sledge load of furniture cannot follow him.' And on communications and high-speed travel, he was equally unimpressed: 'Our inventions are wont to be pretty toys, which distract our attention from serious things. They are but improved means to an unimproved end, an end which it was already but too easy to arrive at; as railroads lead to Boston or New York. We are in great haste to construct a magnetic telegraph from Maine to Texas; but Maine and Texas, it may be, have nothing important to communicate.'

I don't think Thoreau would be on Facebook were he alive today, and his wish to escape the endless swirl would be even stronger. To the city dweller, the sea's appeal grows ever more appealing with every new supermarket, every tweet and every telephone conversation with a call centre. But it has a timeless magic too, and represents something more powerful than just the opportunity to escape from information and overpriced coffee for a while. It can be found in the brilliant orchestral scores that accompany old Technicolor sea movies that proliferated in the 1950s, after the world waged a war on the oceans and returned home filled with their magic. The composers felt the need to use the deepest horns, the most shimmering glissandos of strings, the eeriest of percussion, in an attempt to voice its unknown magic. The sea contains most of life on earth and today, as we never tire of hearing, its floor is less known to us than the surface of the moon – although the main reason is that it's covered in water and therefore invisible. But it is true that fewer have travelled to the bottom of the deepest ocean than have been into space: in fact, only two men have ever visited the deepest point on earth.

It was in 1960 that a Swiss man, Jacques Piccard, and an American, Lt Don Walsh, sank to the bottom of Challenger Deep in the Pacific Ocean, in an Italian submarine termed a bathyscaphe, a word bathed in the redolence of monsters of the deep, Jacques Cousteau and the theme from *Jaws*. They sank down over a period of more than three hours and spent a little time hovering cautiously above the bottom of the world, peering out into a perfect blackness pierced only by the submarine's lamps and the tiny 5-inch-thick Plexiglass window of their barrel, the only material known that was transparent and also able to withstand the 8-tons-per-square-inch pressure down there.

They had been down 36,000 ft, or 11 km, or 7 miles, a mile and a half deeper than Everest is tall. Their sighting of two white flatfish led to their important discovery: that vertebrate life could exist even here, which meant that most of the world that we live in today, at least by volume, is unknown to us. In the half-century since then, no one has ever returned, although it was announced in early 2012 that four teams are planning a descent: among them are Richard Branson of hot-air balloon fame and James Cameron, who got a taste of the deeps on a visit to the real wreck site of the *Titanic*. Now they glory in the faded pre-space-race glamour of their new moniker: they are aquanauts.

It was those nearly bottomless depths I was thinking about that dark night on the Celtic Sea, that immense feeling of eternity, mass and future – the future of science perhaps, certainly exploration – below us. The sea has mystery, but, more than the sheer mass and opportunity of discovery below, more than the micro-organic life glittering and sweeping along the teak decks by our feet, it's the sea's ever-changing surface that gives it its lifeless anima. Waves don't really live of course, but allegorically, and at least with one foot in the objective world of science, they are alive. The wave embodies many of the identifying signatures of life: movement, birth and death. An ocean wave is made not of water, but of the energy that propagates through it.

Waves on the surface of a sea eradicate history, leaving only a restless presence and an unsure future. Steering a boat in tune with their power that night, with the sonar blinking out our depth as it bounced echoes off the ocean floor, and the GPS communing with heavenly bodies to pinpoint our position on the earth, reminded me of the early years playing on the power station wave; one of those moments when the world and man's ability to synthesise it seemed to sound in perfect counterpoint.

Coming off watch that night was a shocking end to my thoughts on the romance of going to sea in small boats. Eight of us, nearly the entire crew complement of that boat, shared a cabin 8 ft by 8 ft by about 7 ft high, where at any time four of us would sleep in bunks stacked two high. After a week, the dank mixture of eight men deprived of a shower or change of clothes, wet oilskins and a hundred farts, had combined to create a stench so powerful that the air felt viscous to breathe. 'Animals – no standards,' muttered Mike, an ex-fighter pilot, as the two of us struggled out of our waterproofs at four in the morning, holding on as the ship heeled from the wind. He was referring to the other two on our watch, who'd slipped to bed gleefully idle and fully dressed. Jimi, the Kiwi bosun of the boat, got out of our bunk so I could get in. 'I flipped the pillow, mate,' he explained, 'so you dribble into your side and flip it over for me when you're done.' He disappeared into the black companionway, leaving me to sleep my four allotted hours. As journalists, we don't do these things because they are easy, I reflected grimly. We do them because they are free.

If the oceans of the world are the planet's basso profondo, the never-ending deep sound of a powerful force in endless circulation, then the rivers are the solo strings, little narrative riffs that start, swell and die away again. The sea appeals to the philosopher, the voyager and the maker of his own destiny. But the river appeals to the storyteller because it is a story in itself, a predetermined tale of beginning, middle and end. The sea enables you to travel anywhere, in any direction. With a river, there's only one way down, yet for all that, a river still has mystery. Look at the sea and you know it goes everywhere and nowhere. But a river, contrary to what many assume, does not always end in the sea or start in the hills. Many start in a reservoir and end in a lake, or start underground, emerge, then dive back under to enter a sewer. The narratives of rivers' lives are many and diverse, but all of them, unlike the sea or the canals, have a destination. The canal has no mystery, no depths, no current and no direction. But, like the river, it does at least have a new surprise waiting around every bend.

Later that morning, corrugated square tubes of coloured sheet steel crossed the canal, feeding into a sinister and substantial brick building on the left-hand side. It was only when I returned home that I discovered that this was the disused Acton Lane Power Station, another ghostly relic of London's days of power. It was a frightening place of negative energy, the opposite of its former self and well used as the setting of the 1986 film *Aliens*.

By lunchtime, I was rowing the little Storm 15 under the graffiti-splattered pillars that uphold an elevated section of the Great Western Avenue, which is the nearest a motorist in London comes to flying, tearing over the western suburbs, looking down on the buildings and enjoying the last light of the day, headlights in the gloaming while the streets below are in darkness. Down here in strong daylight, it was a sharp world of shadow and light as we carried on towards Camden.

Camden was not a friendly place. It made me uneasy, and it took me a while to realise that it was because the ferocious, steep-sided canalside development here has removed any place of refuge where I could stop and pull the boat up. I felt as marginalised and funnelled as those creatures that jumped into the canal and could not get out again. At Camden Lock, knots of young gongoozlers gathered to stand and stare, mute. I tried to place them in a context of relaxed onlookers, but there was something unengaged about their voyeurism. Not one caught my eye or offered help or companionship. I met a woman coming up through a lock from the other direction who said she'd started early in order to pass through Camden, as she couldn't stand the gawping, which apparently worsens as the day wears on. I knew how she felt. Like a hangover, though, the pressing eyes and walls of Camden soon passed and the land opened out again.

My stop that night was the London Canal Museum, one of Britain's many small, volunteer-run transport museums struggling for money in a world that is increasingly uninterested in dusty old things like canals. I had been to see one of the volunteers there a few weeks before, a man who had the air of one embarrassed by his own enthusiasm for his hobby. We had wandered around the museum for a while, two fellow transport enthusiasts, and he had offered me a berth for the boat and a patch of concrete for the night to pitch my tent. A Thermarest self-inflating sleeping mat softens even concrete and soon I had my head down, the lullaby to that night the rumbling and shaking of nearly every tube line in London converging on King's Cross.

A week spent alone in a small boat, in scenery that was at best subtle and in a situation that was less than challenging, gave me plenty of time to think. Quite reasonably, a few friends asked me what I did think about for all that time, and this is quite a personal question. It could be rephrased as, 'Please show me the inside of your soul – not the stuff you talk about – but the secret stuff, deep within.' The answer is rather mundane. When I wasn't worrying about the future of Britain's economy without a 'manufacturing base', the relics of which were so evident all around, I did a lot of counting: how many oar strokes I would make in a mile (500), how many times a heart might beat in its lifetime (about three billion) and the total load-carrying capacity of the Storm 15 based on its buoyancy borne of wood and air (pass). People I knew had been sprouting beastly bits ever since I'd met Frank, which was a constant source of amusement. It meant that I passed by seminal landmarks of the city with something less than the awe they should rightfully have commanded. At Regent's Park Zoo, for instance, I was looking for more animal inspiration for my monstrous creations, and any canal nut would have despaired of the minor historical treasures I undoubtedly missed while lost in reverie or, occasionally, bent double in laughter at some private joke.

Leaving King's Cross the next morning, aware that I was drowning in thoughts about water, I made a conscious effort to think about something else and ran through various non-boat-related memories of a childhood in 1980s London: the theme from *Knight Rider*; collecting coppers for penny sweets; the way Marty McFly kicked the tail down on his skateboard to pick it up and never quite mastering it in the same way; Paula Abdul; not being allowed to see *Fatal Attraction*; the Sherbet Fountain; *Flashdance* (which I was allowed to see, despite it being a '15'); Kim Wilde, largely forgotten and whom every teenage boy in the land was deeply in love with; the Mouse Trap board game; 7-inch B-side remixes, the video for *Take on Me*; the first wooden-bodied video games consoles; MacGyver's home-made bombs; *Choose Your Own Adventure* books; Our Price records – and that bit from *Stand by Me* when the four boys reach a single-track railway line crossing a river valley, a valley that they must cross in order to find a dead body to get their names in the papers. They pause, and the young River Phoenix asks: 'Does anyone know when the next train is coming?'

That was the memory playing as I approached the Islington Tunnel. The Islington Tunnel is nearly 200 years old and nearly three-quarters of a mile long, running under the streets of London in complete and utter darkness, its brick walls damp and dripping. From one end, the half-circle of light at the other end was about the size of a fingernail. In the days of canal transport, the men on narrowboats would lie on the roof of the cabin and walk the boat through by running on their sides like irritable babies, their feet against the slimy black wall. My alternative was the trusty little air-cooled four-stroker. The problem with the Islington tunnel is simple: there is only enough space for one boat to pass. The usual procedure is to come to the mouth of the tunnel, have a good long look to check if anyone's coming, and if the path is clear, proceed. If the path isn't clear, wait.

A narrowboat or a barge is easy to see coming – a large shape with a single Cyclops headlight hammering out a rough jig in diesel; a small dinghy with a nervous man holding a torch? Not so sure. And here was another problem: the darkness of the tunnel meant that I would not be able to swerve out of the way of rubbish that would foul the propeller. And it was too narrow to row, as the blades would scrape against the bricks. If I fouled the propeller, it would take a very long time in the darkness to dismount the motor, lay it in the boat, remove the slime by torchlight, remount it and go through the starting procedure again. So my solution was this: in one hand, I held a powerful hammerhead flashgun, the sort that can recharge every second or so. I had no doubt that it would be seen, but it would be a last resort, as in the darkness of the tunnel it would probably blind me temporarily, and I'd have to remain still, floating in the blackness until I could get going again.

It was, in the event, so dark in the tunnel, I could hardly see to steer, let alone see to avoid rubbish. It was an unpleasant feeling. My torch shone off ancient bricks covered with dripping slime. The blackness of the water was complete and perfect. The idea of falling in was inexplicably, unspeakably horrible and the relief I felt at emerging into sunlight at the other end made me feel quite high for a few minutes.

Under oars, I creaked slowly onward to Victoria Park in Hackney. This is one of the prettiest parts of the Regent's Canal, where Hackney's Georgian architecture still clings to the side of the canal; away from the water, so much of it has been corrupted or demolished. By 11 a.m., I was at a prearranged spot in the park where I was to have a picnic with my parents, and my sister, her husband and two-year-old child, Otto, who, given wings, could take over the world.

We had a happy time in our own way, which tends to be boozy and loud. We had cold red wine, champagne, cold meat, potato and mint salad, lentil salad, bread rolls and delicious little home-made savoury tarts made by my sister's husband. I took them up and down the canal for joyrides. They enjoyed this more than I suspected they would, especially my father and sister who, along with Darwin and Nelson before them, are rather prone to seasickness. My mother is a hardier creature and can be conveyed easily over the surface of water. My father, particularly, is a reluctant sailor, a man for whom crossing even the Channel holds apprehension. As a child, I dragged him around the London Boat Show every January in the hope that he'd buy a family yacht and take us all sailing to far-off places, skipping school for desert islands and London for the world. Much later, by the time I'd discovered that families who do this base their entire existence around such adventures, his mother told me a story about how he'd gone sailing with a schoolfriend and his father back in the 1950s, a trip which involved a grounding on the notorious Goodwin Sands and a crossing of the Thames Estuary under darkness without lights, two things that would make the blood of any sailor run cold.

By the time the noisy gaggle left us it was... horror! Half past three in the afternoon. And I was half-cut.

CHAPTER 12

THE STEAMING SPIRES OF COMMERCE

Victoria Park to Limehouse
Basin, along Regent's Canal:
three miles, sixteen bridges,
four locks, a smaller relic of
steam and a place of refuge.

*Ships are the nearest things to dreams
that hands have ever made.*

ROBERT N. ROSE

I needed to be at Limehouse Basin that evening, a yacht marina in one of the grand old docks of east London, the grandest as far I was concerned, because it is the junction for the Regent's Canal where I was now, the London River where I was going – and the very seldom used Limehouse Cut I'd be rowing down next to get there. There was some distance to go and quite a few locks: for the past 20 miles or so, I'd been 50 ft up on the inner face of the city's bowl, having climbed the Hanwell Flight earlier on. Now, it was time to rejoin the river and it hadn't altered its altitude – which meant I had as many locks still to descend. I started the motor and sped away at all of 3 miles per hour.

The drink had taken its toll, and I was operating the locks slowly and clumsily, getting things in the wrong order and carrying on in much the same way as I had at the beginning of the canals. The canalside was busier here, though: the occasional dog walker and jogger were replaced by small groups of children crowding around. They were friendly and occasionally persistent, one of them asking who I was calling when I picked up a call on my phone by one of the locks. Another of them, a boy of about twelve or so, wanted to know how to work the locks so we tackled one together, but only one, as either he felt he'd got the knack after the first one (it's not complicated after all) or got fed up of running back and forth as I continually left windlasses in the wrong places and tied the boat up wrong, so he left me to it. Amazingly, a little girl approached me soon after this and asked me what it was, pointing at the boat. She can't have been older than ten or so and I didn't think she wanted the lecture about gunter-rig and plywood construction, so I told her, cautiously, that it was a sailing boat. I watched her reaction carefully, wondering if she would find me condescending. *I know that, stupid...* But she still looked dumbfounded. 'It's a little boat you sail and row for fun,' I tried, then talked to her straight. 'Have you never seen a sailing boat or a rowing boat before?' She just shook her head, and then asked, 'Can I come for a ride with you in it?' Now, boat people are as zealous as God people, and we love to convert non-believers just as much. I did want to take her for a ride, but I just shook my head and made an excuse that it was dangerous and I'd have to ask her parents. At the mention of danger, she nodded in dutiful disappointment. I hadn't told her the truth, though. What I was really thinking was that, in Britain, in 2009, if we went for a row, her parents would assume I was a paedophile and call the police or attack me. I rowed away, disappointed to have acquiesced to such a distorted idea, but buoyed by a much happier truth. Kids don't sail, or find some other way of leaving the world behind walls, only because they don't know how to – not because they don't want to.

The architecture was getting comically ugly now, as One Canada Square, better known as Canary Wharf Tower, appeared in the distance; a tall, high rectangle, straight out of a school geometry textbook, wearing a silly triangular hat. At night, the ambition of the people working inside forces its way out of the top as steam, clearly visible from ground level on a still night, lit up by the building's flashing light at the top. I do wonder why London's skyline is becoming phallic and representational. One of the most popular buildings of recent years was 30 St Mary Axe (*Look! It's like a gherkin!*). Soon, the Shard will have a similar appeal (*Look, it's so... tall!*). Like Canary Wharf, they do not seem to reflect any ideology. The Gherkin, though, if it can't embody an idea, embodies a pickled snack, so it at least has an air of whimsical fun.

In the foreground was a slim, octagonal, brick-built tower resembling a monumental obelisk. This was, in fact, another power station, but of a different kind. The 1869 Limehouse Accumulator Tower is a relic from the days when Limehouse was a centre of the lime trade, burning limestone in kilns for use in just about everything from agriculture to early forms of mortar to stick bricks together. The tower would be filled with water, and a 100-ton weight would be raised by the power of a coal boiler to sit on top, pressurising the water and providing hydraulic power to the cranes by the river, via a network of pipes. It also provided power to the lifts of local offices and hotels until as late as 1977, when it was finally closed. The pipes were later filled with communications cables instead, finding a new role in London's fiendishly complex and secretive underground utilities network.

The canal had become bright green and choked with algae now, the soft, sticky weed dripping from my oars and slowing me down further, and the sun was low as I finally slinked into Limehouse at 6.30 p.m., going through the last lock with the help of a thin, scruffy man in his forties, walking with an Alsatian that looked more like a wolf on a bad hair day. He told me he lives on a boat in Limehouse with some friends. In fact, he was waiting for his home to come through the lock then, which is why he was there, windlass dangling from one hand in the classic lockside boater's pose, just as I was.

Limehouse Basin felt like a fitting finale to the days spent on the canals. It was one of London's first docks to close in the 1960s, and its redevelopment into a marina and residential area has worked comparatively well. The buildings fringing the edge are in sympathetic proportion and the boats tied up to the floating wooden pontoons are an interesting mixture of seagoing yachts and narrowboats from the canals, giving the place the feel of a crossroads. At the inland end, the end I'd just come from, the little red-and-blue trains of the Docklands Light Railway, built to serve the regenerated Docklands in the 1980s, clatter over an old viaduct, built in the old yellow brick of London that seems to glow when the sun shines on it. It was built by no less a character than George Stephenson, builder of the world's first railway.

The basin is also home to the Cruising Association, the red-brick clubhouse headquarters of a worldwide fraternity of cruising sailors, with a warren of rooms for visiting yachtsmen and, downstairs, one of London's friendliest bars, provided you are ready to talk about the magic of the seven seas, the battery drain of an electronic watermaker, what a pain marine fridges are (there is always a story of waiting for spare parts for a fridge in some far-off port) and the relative merits of different anchorages around the islands of the Caribbean. I don't know a great deal about this sort of blue-water, round-the-world-with-aircon sailing, but it's usually practised by retired couples not content with gardening, reading or playing with the grandchildren. In any event, despite the penalty of the odd fridge-spare-part story, the bar is a friendly little oasis, a house filled with the excitement of voyages ended and the next horizon.

I found my berth easily, tied up and headed ashore to the bar. I downed a pint of cold beer standing, at the sort of speed that is usually followed directly by slamming the glass down on the counter and shouting 'Hit me!' at the bartender. I took another one to a table to drink more slowly, collapsing gloriously into the comfortable novelty of a deeply upholstered chair. A few tables away, a group of three men were sat, watching the new arrival. They looked more 'fridge spare parts' than 'magic of the seven seas', so I pulled my phone out and pretended to look busy for a while, while the bar woman went to look for the keys to my room.

This was a big moment in the trip. Halfway in one sense, though with the tide to carry me back to my starting place I only had three days left on the water. My cousin was going to join me the next day but had to cancel, so we agreed he'd join me for a day on the river later instead. And that meant a day off tomorrow, before my friend Julian joined me the day after to sail out through the Barrier before heading back into central London. But that night at least, it was time for a bath, a hot meal and a night in the pub with people I actually knew. Louise, a colleague, lived on a speedboat in the basin and her Dutch boatbuilder boyfriend was in town. We went out and drank beer for a while, comparing our favourite nautical books as we sat by the river. After a while, they left to eat at a Chinese restaurant nearby, and I declined, not sure if my presence was wanted, and not sure if I could make any more decent conversation. They wanted to know about my journey and I couldn't, for some reason, put it into any meaningful words. And I couldn't think of anything else to talk about either.

I walked to the river's edge to watch the sun set. The Thames was rolling by placidly, still emptying out, but slowly now, at the end of a tide and losing energy. I wandered the few hundred yards to my accommodation for the night, a cosy little cabin with a soft, clean bed, a shared bathroom and a fridge, toaster, sink and washing machine outside in the hall; everything a visiting yachtsman or the master of a small dinghy needs. Before turning in for the night I turned around at the top of the stairwell and saw a large photo of Sir Robin Knox-Johnston staring at me from a poster. The Cruising Association celebrated its centenary that year, and RKJ took the post of president for the year. Forty years after sailing around the world non-stop and alone, he was watching over my miniature adventure around London.

CHAPTER 13

THE REAL CIRCLE LINE

```
Limehouse Basin: catching up
on beer, company and sleep —
and a ride on the tube.
```

I feel sorry for people who don't drink.
They wake up in the morning and that's
the best they're going to feel all day.

FRANK SINATRA

It's not often you can find a hole in the middle of the week, leaving you to disappear through it and land in a world of temporary idleness. I got up around 10 a.m. and walked around the basin, looking at the boats, rank after rank of yachts, powerboats and narrowboats tied up to the wooden pontoons, many of them in the white glass-reinforced plastic (GRP) that took over from wood in the 1960s. GRP is not, as it's commonly assumed, the superior successor to wood for boatbuilding. It has virtually no insulation against the cold, it sweats condensation in the cabin, and through its thin walls you can hear everything. It is also heavier than wood for its strength, meaning a modern wooden boat is lighter and faster than its equivalent in GRP. Wood is also stiffer. The problem with wood is that it's hard to maintain. Keeping an old wooden boat can sometimes feel, as a friend once put it, like trying to keep a grand piano in your back garden.

Wooden boats are built of... well, wood, which is an expensive material that is turned from planks into a boat by skilled craftsmen – and their depreciation is frightening. A new 30-ft wooden yacht will cost three times as much as a plastic boat to buy, and within a decade it will be worth less than half the value of that plastic boat. Second-hand wooden boats, consequently, are a steal. £10,000 or less will buy a beautiful 25-ft cruising yacht with four berths in a cosy cabin, a little shell that will take you anywhere you care to sail. Another blessing of a wooden boat, though, is that it is wonderfully recyclable. A dead wooden boat can be turned into furniture or, at worst, burned for warmth in winter. Even if just left to its own devices, languishing on the mud somewhere, it will slowly return to its element of earth as it rots away – ashes to ashes and dust to dust.

GRP boats are easier to maintain and cheaper to buy, being made out of poison and pressed out in moulds. At the end of their lives, they sit in their hundreds up every creek and river and marina in the land. The owner might have stopped using the boat years ago, and he's still paying his yearly mooring fee. What else can he do? It's too strong to break up and too big to take to the tip. If you really don't like someone, leave him a yacht in your will.

I walked to a petrol station, filled the green plastic can with fuel and walked back to the little Storm 15 lying among the ranks of blinding white plastic. I went to find Jeremy to give him the spare lock windlass that had come with me from Brentford at the Grand Union Canal's western confluence with the Thames. Jeremy was as quiet, studious and gentle as always. He is surely the laureate of all lock-keepers, with not only a keen interest in history but also, I discovered, in sailing.

We walked around to his pontoon berth and boarded his boat, a well-maintained little 25-ft cruising yacht. We ducked under the companionway and took a seat each on the saloon berths, a sofa running down each side of the cabin that can be used to sleep or sit on. There is a glorious profusion of junk on a yacht this size. With no space to hide it, the owner is forced to turn his life inside out for anyone who might care to see it. Frying pans, a half-full bottle of washing-up liquid and a pair of navigation dividers shared one outcrop while, on another, lifejackets were piled high with pilot books stacked on top as a scruffy, leaning finial.

Nowhere was there room to stand and at the aft end was a tiny galley on one side and, on the other, the saloon berth extended backwards under the cockpit seat, into a sort of hidden bunk called a quarter berth. At the bows, forward of where the mast came through from the deck above, was a netted-off area containing clothing, bedding and all manner of paraphernalia peculiar to little yachts like these, coastal yachts, designed for weekend sailing not too far from the shore, and with a low draught able to sail in the shallow waters of areas like the East Coast, which is where Jeremy's next trip was planned for.

The East Coast is, along with the Solent, West Country and the west coast of Scotland, fabled among British yachtsmen, largely because of its proximity to London, making an escape from the city to the big skies and mudflats a possibility, even if just for a weekend. From the 1950s on, sailing writers based there, like the famous Maurice Griffiths, wrote books with subtitles like 'an introduction for the man in the city'. The 'East Coast' (note the reverential capital letters) does not mean, as it does to a landsman, the right-hand side of England, or Britain. The East Coast means, more specifically, the greater Thames Estuary, running from the grand, forgotten town of Ramsgate in the south, sticking out into the North Sea on England's knuckle, up to Ipswich in Suffolk. It is made up of the counties of Kent, Essex and Suffolk, and, though just a stone's throw from London, is unknown to most Londoners, apart from the fortunate few, sailors in the main, who have discovered it. It's a land of endless rivers, creeks and salt marshes, with little towns and villages that time left behind, because the future belonged to the metropolis 30 miles upriver, and to cheap holidays in Spain. The coastal villages of Suffolk and Essex have found some cachet with the London crowd, but the grand seaside frontages, esplanades and cobbled villages of the Kent coast have been so forgotten they might never have existed. Londoners are more likely to have climbed Mount Kilimanjaro than visited the towns of Deal, Sandwich or Faversham.

In March of 2007, I spent the chilly first week of March on the Suffolk coast learning how to sail and navigate a yacht on a work trip to teach me, the new recruit to the magazine, to sail. There were five of us squeezed onto a classic 32-ft wooden racing sloop of 1950s vintage, a time when it seems everyone must have been much thinner and less reliant on creature comfort, judging by the width of the bunks. We cruised up and down the freezing brown rivers past leafless trees, seeking comfort in warm pubs every night and waking up early every morning with bursting bladders, hot heads and red faces. We travelled down the River Orwell, from the beautiful little hamlet called Pin Mill, the place the Walker kids sailed from in the Arthur Ransome classic, *We Didn't Mean to Go to Sea*. That, written in the late 1930s, was in the day when it would have been a wild place, peopled by sailing bargemen, the last men and boats to trade under sail in Britain – the full stop on a sentence thousands of years long. The Thames barges were masterful designs. Around 80 ft or so long, beamy and with a rounded shape, they had flat bottoms, enabling them to settle upright on the seabed when the tide went out. Their distinctive brown mainsails don't have booms running along their bottom edge, but instead, a sprit, a wooden spar running from the bottom of the mast to the outboard tip of the quadrilateral sail, and that sprit used to double as a loading derrick when the boats were taking on or unloading cargo. They are remembered in paintings of the time and in literature, particularly in the work of Dickens, and T. S. Eliot, who returned repeatedly to the Thames in *The Waste Land*: 'The river sweats oil and tar, the barges drift with the turning tide, red sails wide to leeward swing on the heavy spar.' They were the Ford Transits of their day, thousands of the vessels plying their way not just around the Thames Estuary but all around the British coast, and a good number of them still exist, owned by enthusiasts who charter them to day trippers and/or live on them. They kept trading under sail until after the war and, for transportation of dynamite, considered too risky a load for the vibration, sparks and heat of an engine, well into the 1960s. Today, to sail past the mouth of the River Orwell into the North Sea is to sail with giants. At Felixstowe Container Port, the deep-water superlative of the ports of London, Tilbury and Felixstowe, ocean-going container ships are manoeuvred into place by tugs with the slow invisibility of the hour hand of a clock.

My friend Darryl joined me later in the evening. He said he couldn't stay out too late as he had work the next day but as we sat by the open window in London's best pub, The Grapes, with the warm night air blowing in, and the river, at high tide, lapping the building's 300-year-old bricks outside, and the lights of the riverbank opposite shining in the darkness, thoughts about work were quickly forgotten, and we slowly worked our way through far too much beer, the water from the river occasionally slapping up the wall outside and splashing onto our table, warm and clear through the open windows. The river gets its brownness only from its mass, strength in numbers. In droplets it is clear.

That would have been a good evening to make my odd little discovery about London. In fact, it wasn't until a year later that it struck me, and at that time I was riding on the real Circle Line underground. I didn't know what I'd been hoping to find, but it seemed only right to make a circuit under the city on the tube line the book was named after, and aimlessly riding the Circle Line had an interesting bit of historical precedent: Londoners in the war were for some time prevented from using the platforms of the underground network to shelter from bombs, so many bought the cheapest ticket and spent their days simply travelling around and around in this endless loop.

It struck me that London, at least the London north of the river, is an island created by the waterways of the Grand Union Canal and the Thames which flow around it in one continuous loop: the loop I had been on. Of course, it's an island only in name and it has no bearing on the life of the city, but it had a bearing in the way I thought about the city; it was a way of parcelling it off, of removing myself from it while floating past it from the no-man's-land of water. What really makes London an island more than a thin ribbon of canal is its bowl shape, its dense mass of heat-radiating buildings and the fact that being in London means being indoors. It's a city that weather passes over. When it rains at night, we hardly hear it any more. When the winds howl along the south and east coasts, the tips of the oak trees in London barely move outside your windows at night. The stars hide above a nocturnal, orange haze and if you want to see them you must go to the top of a hill, like Hampstead. When a wild Atlantic weather front grinds in, you hide your face in your scarf and shuffle quickly home. The weather is just another small inconvenience of the day.

On the Circle Line, the real one, London seemed a lonely sort of island, each of us cocooned in a fragile privacy, a privacy not as comfortable or as intense as I felt on the other circle line of water above. Here, the souls of the city's inhabitants are not written on their faces – but some idea of their dreams is fixed to the wall of the carriage just above their heads, on the glossy advertisement cards. Here, the endless story of lack reveals itself. 'Your perfect girl could be sitting right under this ad', read one of them. I looked down – not the perfect girl, but a fat bloke reading the same ad above my head, engaged in a perfect symmetry of disappointment with me that I was not *his* perfect girl. 'We're here just in case she isn't', it went on. 'She's in London somewhere. All you have to do is find her.' This brings forth images of flying over the city at night, peering in through penthouse windows and seeing lovers dancing, merry groups around the piano, cats sitting on windowsills under a cheese moon, parties, jazz, long, loquacious dinner parties with too much wine, swimming eyes, views of the river. Of course, that only happens in movies. Judging by the number of these ads on the tubes nowadays, you might expect to fly through the night sky of the fantasy city and see a series of different people, each alone at a laptop, a thousand Carrie Bradshaws and her male equivalents flying through the lovelorn night digitally, wings replaced by trumped-up statements of romantic compatibility – *hobbies: film, travel, long walks, country pubs, drinking wine by an open fire.* If these agents of Cupid fail, the ad next to the online dating one offers the corollary: 'IVF – free if you're thirty-five or under and willing to share your eggs.' And opposite, an advertisement from a sperm bank appealing to men to spill their seed far and wide for the women who never did find that man who wanted long walks in the country followed by the bottle of wine by the roaring fire. Another board advertised a gym: 'Lighten Up', it punned.

This insularity, the fragile shells we have built around ourselves, has been created by the city itself. The multitudes, and our proximity to each other within those multitudes, have leavened us into creatures of insipid kindness and tepid concern, with a desperate wish to avoid offence. Political correctness has evolved into emotional correctness (*You can't say that!* they utter, shocked), and it's getting harder and harder to speak with any fire or honesty. Legions of young men and women are like everyone and no one, uniquely ordinary, malleable enough to survive this new century of flippant cordiality, master chameleons of adaptability. It would be hard to hate them. But it would be hard to fall in love with them too; the city gently erodes our differences and we have become a jigsaw puzzle of similar pieces. The awkwardly shaped nubs are worn off and the pieces slide off against each other.

CHAPTER 14

DOWN THE INTESTINE

Limehouse Basin to Greenwich
Yacht Club on the Limehouse Cut,
Bow Creek and River Thames. Five
miles, one lock, fifteen bridges.
Sailing down runways, a disaster
at Bow Creek – and the author
has some company on board.

Teach a man to sail and he'll stay out for a day. Give him a wooden boat and you'll never see him again.

ANONYMOUS (ADAPTED)

After checking out of my cabin at the Cruising Association with a thick head and gluey, red eyes, I again walked the few yards to the river's edge, crossing the narrow road filled with commuters on Vespas, black cabs, and big, red, hissing wagon-train buses. After just a few more steps, it was there, as immutable as it ever was, flowing by sedately, a-thrum with its unfeeling motion.

Julian was waiting for me back at the Cruising Association when I walked back across the road. He had only landed in London twelve hours ago, after flying in from Madeira, the Portuguese-owned island in the Atlantic, 500 miles west of the African coast. He'd sailed across the Atlantic (as far as Madeira) to get here and I found him in an upstairs office, chatting to Janet, the administrator at the CA, about her house on Madeira, the oldest house on the island. It's been in her family for centuries, and in the back garden there grows a tree that was planted by Captain Cook on one of his exploratory voyages around the world in the late eighteenth century.

Julian and I made our way down to the boat and stepped in gingerly, the little Storm 15 threatening to tip us into the marina. Julian took the oars and I sat at the tiller, and slowly we made our way down out of the marina and down the Limehouse Cut towards Bow Creek. It's a short waterway, built in 1776 to connect the River Lea, that place of fly fishing, poison and industry, to Limehouse Basin, there giving access to the Grand Union Canal or the Thames, but avoiding the tortuously winding last reach of the River Lea, the tidal Bow Creek, which was our route out of the canal system.

Julian is a good guide to the Thames – and, for that matter, London. An architect and obsessive yacht sailor, he was born in Gravesend on the river's edge, and spent his boyhood repairing boats on the Thames. He's at least 150 years old, wears the sort of glasses that enable not just enhanced sight but the solving of insoluble problems, and has a grey beard that can sense barometric pressure. Right now, he was explaining the cable bridges crossing this urban little cut of water, buildings rising up either side, leaving no room for a footpath. A moment later, he squinted up at an aeroplane and started explaining its angle of descent towards London City Airport and its noise implications – he had something to do with the viability study for the airport when it was first mooted in the early 1980s as part of the redevelopment of London's old docklands. I can't pretend I entirely understand everything Julian speaks of, so I won't try to relate the story now, but London City Airport is an exciting place to fly out of on a clear day, the entire patchwork of islands, rivers and mudflats of the Thames Estuary visible below, as you fly east to continental Europe. It's an even more exciting place to sail past.

The airport, which opened in 1988, was built along the side of the Royal Albert Dock, which forms a continuous line of water with the Victoria Dock. These are, by far, the biggest of London's enclosed docks and building them out of the marshes of east London took sixty-six years, between 1855 and 1921. The water in them provided a natural spirit level ensuring that the docks could only be absolutely flat. In the same way that the level, straight canals enabled the railways that often ran alongside them, these docks enabled jet travel. They dwarf not only the other old London docks, but also the newer Tilbury Docks downriver, built to replace them. It has to be a clear day to be able to see from one end to the other, because they are 2.5 miles long, which made them in their day the largest docks in the world.

In 2007, I helped deliver a 100-year-old Thames sailing barge from where it was moored at the Victoria Dock, upriver into central London. Navigation along the Victoria Dock is very tightly regulated, for just a few hundred feet away, running alongside, is the airport's runway, just over a third of the length of the docks that preceded it. We had dispensation to go, and as we chugged along under the old diesel, we could hear the scream of jet engines building over our heads and the little squeals of tyres as the Boeings and Airbuses touched down onto the runway with a puff of burning rubber. It was hair-raisingly exciting, each one building slowly from a distance, the white-noise jet sound growing and growing until it was a glorious scream, the most powerful sound of the twentieth century, drowning out the clattering diesel, our voices and the thoughts in our heads.

Once we were out in the river, the boat's owner asked me if I knew how to steer a Thames barge. These boats are around 80 ft long and weigh the best part of 100 tons. To steer, at least on this particular Thames barge, you stand on the very end part of the stern and use a wheel, as opposed to a tiller, which you find on smaller boats. This position near the very end of the boat enables you to glance down and see the position of the rudder, which extends above the water as well as below it. The idea, as Alan, for that was his name, pointed out to me, was to glance over from time to time to see if it was straight or not. Keen not to miss out on the chance to steer one of these great little ships upriver, I replied that I did indeed know how to steer a Thames barge, thinking it couldn't be that much harder than steering a yacht and guessing that he might have been asking the question in the same spirit as a salt asks a greenhorn if he knows the difference between port and starboard. It was a raw January day, and Alan went below to rustle up some lunch in the boat's huge hold, converted to a cosy galley and cabins. I'd figure it out.

I discovered very quickly that I could only make the boat go like a snake, weaving from one side of the river to the middle and back, scattering lesser vessels in its path. Narrowboats, yachts and sailing dinghies all had to spring to the banks or into the middle of the river as they saw the drunken giant bearing down on them. The problem was the time that the boat took catching up to alterations in the steering, which meant constant over-correction on my part. For twenty minutes or so, we continued on this dangerous, serpentine course until Alan came back on deck, a bowl of soup in each hand, and took the wheel again.

Later, I experienced the size of the Victoria Dock without a boat, swimming a mile around it as part of a charity swim, in the leisurely time of forty minutes. About three thousand of us had turned up to swim in these filthy waters, all dressed in black neoprene wetsuits as the rules of the race demanded. Far from glorious competitors, we were a mass of undesirable oddballs, the cheering crowds replaced by small groups of the loving and the patient. The water was warm, making the wetsuits an unnecessary hindrance, but the taste of the water was venomous – thick, dark and metallic, it was foul enough to make the Thames outside a spring of clear meltwater by comparison. In length, the Victoria and Royal Albert Docks would stretch from King's Cross Station in north London all the way to Borough Market south of the river. To Londoners, who view their city as the world, it is the equivalent of going abroad. Our circular swimming course of 1 mile occupied only a tiny corner of the docks.

Back on the Limehouse Cut, we'd moved off the topic of passenger jet landing-approach angles and onto the rather more domestic subject of people who lie on their mobile phones, as in 'I've just passed King's Cross and I'll be home in a minute' when they are, in fact, stuck in traffic miles from home in Oxford Circus. The shock is not the lie itself, but the brazenness of announcing it to a bus full of people sat in silence, in the middle of Oxford Circus.

Two days ago, Julian was in the company of flying fish, warm trade winds, sperm whales and tropical islands on his transatlantic sail, but seemed quite rejuvenated to be back in his beloved east London, as we rowed the last few yards to Bow Locks. One of Jeremy's colleagues from the Limehouse Lock had arrived by foot to open the lock, by prearrangement. The lock is manned only by arrangement and, these days, very seldom used. The big Victorian doors swung open just as the river outside rose to its full height, and we free-flowed out of a living, breathing museum, straight onto Bow Creek. Bow Creek, which is the last section of the River Lea, is one of the most winding sections of river I have ever seen. For years, it scythed its way through the soft silt, building sharper and sharper meanders until the sides were embanked and now, like the Thames in London, has rather been caught with its pants around its ankles. It would love to straighten itself out and desert its curves as a series of stagnant oxbow lakes, but it can't; it is caught going around in circles forever. From the air it looks like a lower intestine, which is pretty much what it was in its nineteenth-century heyday of the Industrial Revolution, when it would funnel the toxins from the River Lea into the Thames.

It took us the best part of two hours to row the 2.5 miles down Bow Creek to the mouth of the Thames, two points just a mile away from each other as the crow flies. Julian rowed most of the way, keen, perhaps, to exercise his muscles in his natural environment after being cooped up in a pressurised jetliner cabin.

Bow Creek might have been the drabbest place I'd been so far on my journey, but it has a history steeped in shipbuilding, premiership football, and one of the worst, and most unlikely, ship disasters ever to happen on the Thames and its tributaries. Exactly what happened on 21 June 1898 has sometimes been misunderstood by the admittedly small group of historians who claim knowledge of it, despite its thorough documentation in the newspapers of the day and, more surprisingly, film archive taken at the time.

Thames Ironworks, at the mouth of Bow Creek, had been in a period of decline for some years, with the shipbuilding yards of the north and Scotland, like those on the Clyde, taking over most of the business. The firm had recently been bought by a munificent Victorian entrepreneur, Arnold Hills. His particular formula to life revolved around vegetarianism, hard work and sport. He'd played football while at Oxford and set up a football club for the shipbuilders, which would eventually become West Ham FC. He also cut the working day of his employees from twelve hours to eight. What with that and the building of the HMS *Albion*, things must have seemed good at Thames Ironworks during the last few years of the twentieth century. *Albion* was an iron warship of 14,000 tons. Metal ships had come late to the Royal Navy and the French had gained a lead in their manufacture, building vessels of fearsome modernity – 'novel ships of formidable power', as an admiral of the Navy of the time phrased it.

HMS *Albion* would settle the score with those frog-devouring upstarts and when the day of the launch arrived, a crowd of 100,000 (*East Ham Echo*), or at least 'an unusually large number' (*The Times*) of spectators, had gathered to watch the launch, along with the Duke and Duchess of York. Many of these were the wives and children of the men who worked at the yard.

According to some sources, the Duchess swung the champagne bottle on the prow of the ship and it refused to break, a terrible omen to those who believe in them. She swung twice more and on all three occasions, the glass refused to shatter. What happened next is unclear. The ship was launched, but not, as some maintain, sideways, which would certainly better explain what followed. She slid in gently, stern first, and, within moments, a displacement wave ran ashore gathering in size as it went, demolishing a makeshift walkway and sweeping into the water the hundred or more people who had been standing there for a better view of the launch. Their screams as they fought each other, their clothing, the timbers of the broken pier, the muddy waters and their inability to swim, were set against the backdrop of happy cheering and applause, their plight passing unnoticed in the heat of the occasion.

Thirty-eight of them drowned, mostly women and children from the local area, among the poorest inhabitants of London. The wave was described by the *East Ham Echo* as 'nine or ten foot high', which is a landsman's fantasy. The biggest displacement waves on the Thames, usually caused by the wash of passing boats, act out in miniature the same cycle as tsunamis, surf waves or any energy waves that move through water. They grow in height as they feel the bottom shallowing under them at the gently sloping edges of the river, but never do they grow to this dimension, which, in surfer's terminology, is more than a 'double overhead' – over twice the height of the surfer in his ride stance. As *The Times* put it at the time, 'accounts differ as to what actually happened'.

The result was the same whatever the size of the wave. As the night wore on, the quayside pile of hats and coats and umbrellas grew, and hysterical husbands queued up looking for their wives and children among the dead. A week later, the bodies were buried, most of them in a communal grave in the nearby neighbourhood of Plaistow. The shock of what happened that day, a day filled with the innocent happiness of the women and children who'd arrived to see the fruit of their men's labours, was very affecting and it's one of the dark river's saddest accidents in a long list. One reported image, whether true or not, took the public imagination and has become part of the folklore of the event. It was the moment a woman was pulled from the murk, unconscious and unbreathing, two dead children still clinging to the hem of her skirt in rigor mortis. She never came around. A popular poet of the time, McGonagall, wrote a report of the event in verse:

> A great crowd had gathered to search for the missing dead,
> And many strong men broke down because their heart with pity bled,

As they looked upon the distorted faces of their
relatives,
While down their cheeks flowed many a silent tear.

It was not just newspapermen and poets who chronicled the happening: two rival film-makers, Robert Paul and E. P. Prestwich, were capturing the event from rowing boats. And today, their footage of the launch can be seen on YouTube: where else? *Albion* went on to fight in the Battle of Gallipoli in World War One and was eventually sold for scrap in 1919.

Finally, after what seemed an interminable series of meanders, we passed under the A13 and reached the mouth of the creek, where a miniature lighthouse stands, the most inland on the Thames and now a museum of its own past. We rowed across the river, a tiny dinghy bobbing on the deep brown swells, surrounded by shipping and heavy industry. A Harbour Authority launch bobbed over to us to check on our well-being, perhaps wondering if we needed a tow to safety, then headed away again upriver. A few minutes later, we'd reached the other side and tied up to the Greenwich Yacht Club to wait for the tide to ebb away to sea before we could ride the flood back into central London.

It felt good to be out of the canals and back on the river. These canals, in hindsight at least, were a mistake – just like everything else we build. Considered today in the light of tomorrow, everything we build, think and assume is a future perfect mistake, at least against the standard we have always strived for: perfection. In time, all will be superseded, the length of an object's or an idea's service usually being the best indicator of how well it did. The canals and locks hadn't done so well. Not so the river, I reflected, as we stepped onto the pontoon of the Greenwich Yacht Club; the river is not expected to be perfect. The river is implacable. It was here before the city and might still be here after it.

CHAPTER 15
WAITING FOR THE TIDE

`Greenwich Yacht Club.`

*I know nothing more imposing than the
view the Thames offers during the ascent
from the sea to London Bridge.*

FREDERICK ENGELS

Three hours might seem quite a long time to hang around, particularly when you consider that Julian and I were not remotely worried by the fact. We had to wait for low water slacks so we could sail downriver a few hundred yards to go through the Thames Barrier before heading into London and we had no plans to do anything other than simply hang around, absorb the sun shining down from a cloudless, dark-blue sky and watch the river, where, just then, a 30,000-ton seagoing ship was unloading crushed rock from Norway on our right. Some low, mean buildings of this more industrialised section of the river sat opposite and, to our left, the squat metallic David Beckham Football Academy.

We've heard a lot about David Beckham, who has become one of the most famous men on the planet over the years. Not so many people remember the Leysdown disaster in August 1912, four months after RMS *Titanic* went to the bottom of the North Atlantic. A 32-ft ex-naval cutter, with twenty-four East London Sea Scouts on board, was en route from Waterloo Bridge to the Isle of Sheppey a few miles further east in London's broad estuary. The boat was laid flat by a squall and nine boys died. Three Beckham boys were on board, including David's great-grandfather, who was one of the survivors. Without his survival, the Lord of Beckingham Palace, sufferer of metatarsal injuries and maestro of free kicks, would never have existed. And we would never have heard of Rebecca Loos.

Later that year, the *Daily Mirror* raised the money to buy the Sea Scouts a 52-ton ketch called *Mirror*. The next year, she was off Gravesend in Kent, again in the estuary, not far from the scene of the Leysdown disaster, when she was run down by the tanker *Hogarth* in heavy fog. This time, four souls were lost. An inquest acquitted the behaviour of those on board *Mirror*, recording their navigation as 'proper and seamanlike'. Fog is still one of the sailor's worst enemies.

It's a peculiar fact that if there's one thing sailors love more than sailing, it's not sailing. This is why we get so excited by landfall: it means getting off the boat. It's the same thing with many fishermen; if there's one thing they love as much as catching fish – it's the only possible alternative: not catching fish. If there's one thing sailors love even more than not sailing, though, it's hanging around boatyards and looking at other people's boats.

Greenwich Yacht Club is London's only yacht club. There are scores of historic rowing clubs and sailing clubs like the one I'd left from. But a traditional yacht club with men working on their yachts propped up on dirty old baulks of timber; dirty white plastic mooring buoys attached to the riverbed by chains; a clubhouse; and a large concrete apron with boats in various stages of repair? There's only one of them. After eating our lunch on the pontoon (more salami, more olives and more blue cheese with beer warmed in the sun), we headed up the jetty to walk around looking at the boats, mostly little sailing yachts in the 20–30-ft range, one of them with a black cab pulled up beside it as the driver tinkered inside the cabin, fitting for a proper London yacht club. I wondered if he had a hectoring wife in Billericay who'd blow her top if she knew that this – *this!* – was what he got up to when he said he was earning money and she was looking after two screaming kids stamping crisps into the carpet and baying for unaffordable toys. Or if he was, like so many wooden boat addicts, already divorced, and planning some day to sail to the Caribbean and the South Sea Islands in the Pacific. Or if he'd been lucky enough to find a woman who shared his passion: perhaps she was down there with him in the cabin, cheerfully painting the deck beams and not minding the glossy paint that dripped down onto her upturned face.

Like so many things in sailing, there is a ritual to looking around a yard full of old yachts, a ritual in which I am a keen amateur, and one that Julian has mastered after his century and a half on this planet. It's a lot more complicated than sailing itself. Hands go into pockets, and walking is done at a slow stroll. Propping a short yellow pencil behind one ear would not be remotely out of place. The wearing of blue overalls, whether necessary or not, would also be tolerated – welcomed even – if fancy permitted.

The art to it, really, is knowing which boats not to bother commenting upon. Some boats you just walk past. It would be in as bad form to comment on a boat's ugliness as it would be to think it worthy of dissection. The only worthwhile comment is a terse, grunted 'Bavaria 38 – hired one of those in the Med once...' So you wander until you come upon a boat that is worthy of a proper verbal essay. First you try to guess what it is; if you don't know, a near miss is good. 'Looks a bit like...' shows you have got it wrong in quite a knowledgeable way. This bit goes on for quite a while, with guesses as to what year it might have been built in, and at which yard, and in what wood. If you have a friend who used to have one, that's even better. Shows you are a living, breathing part of it all, not just a trainspotter.

A blistering performance in Part One would go something like this: 'Ah – it's *Bollo*! Used to have a Hillyard myself – think this is a later one, probably 1950s. Of course

David had run out of pitch pine by then, so it's probably mahogany.' Step up for a closer look. 'Yes, definitely mahogany – but it's not so bad, you know, long as you keep it pickled. I used to know David, you know, back when he was still building them in Littlehampton. Used to sail with him. In fact, you know what?' Step back, misty-eyed. 'I used to sail this one too! Used to belong to Dick – must have had a name change. I wonder how Dick is these days…' A creditable performance might go something like this: 'Looks like a Hillyard – nice boats – good accommodation. Not the fastest, but I've heard they're pretty seaworthy…' Inexcusable performances would be as follows: 'Nice boat! Is it really made of wood?' Or 'Look at that old pile of shit – anyone got a match?' followed by a wistful glance at the average white plastic yacht next to it… 'Now that's more like it.'

Part Two is an assessment of the boat's condition. To get top marks in this category, you'd say something like: 'Oh dear, it's not looking as good as when it was sailing out of Woodbridge. Dick took good care of that little boat.' Take a long look down the hull with one eye shut and murmur something incomprehensible and… magical… under your breath: 'Just starting to go…' Then look at something like the shrouds (the wire stays that hold the mast to the boat) and murmur 'Too tight, too tight.' The trick is then to go to a seemingly completely unrelated part of the boat, like underneath, on all fours, and say something like, 'Yes, it's pulled the garboard out of alignment just a centimetre…

they did that on these old Hillyards. They were trying to get a better windward performance before everyone started adding bowsprits. You see this on a lot of them.' Then suggest the cure, which must sound completely unrelated to the problem: 'Nothing a bit of Stockholm tar won't sort out.' A creditable performance might concentrate on the surface of the vessel – a generic comment on rubbing down wood and varnishing would suffice here – just. A wide-eyed remark like 'Is someone really going to fix that?!' would constitute a fail at this point in the proceedings.

The final part of the assessment concerns the boat's qualities as a sailing vessel. Unlike in Part One, experience of sailing a boat of its type (or that very vessel), is not necessarily an advantage. Better than that is the confident assessment of how it would sail based purely on measuring the hull and rig with the eye of experience. After all, if you've sailed it, you already know. This is probably the easiest part of the performance. You look at the bows, the way the boat enters the water, the stern, the way it might break up a following sea, the overall shape and the rig. Noticing how the sails are reefed gets brownie points, and noting that all the sail being carried on one mast would make the boat a 'handful' is quite respectable, if not *de rigueur*. The keen enthusiast can make up a bit of ground here that he lost earlier, just by noting that the roller reefing on the headsails might make life a bit easier for the single-handed sailor. The novice will say something like 'How many people could sleep in the cabin?' not realising that real sailors, being real men of course, affect complete indifference to any pointless creature comforts like the ability to sleep and eat.

A watched kettle never boils and a watched tide never turns, but after a while trailing around the boatyard, low water was approaching and we wandered back down the jetty to the pontoon where the little Storm 15 was waiting. Our time to head downriver for the Barrier was nigh. The Barrier asks questions about permanency and our place on water. The course of a river is a symbol of implacability and its tides the allegory of time itself. Time and tide wait for no man, as the truism goes. It's not Shakespeare or Chaucer, though it's sometimes attributed to one or other – like many things connected to water, it's beyond written history's reach. But the river has been altered, compromised and perverted throughout its history like nowhere else on earth. Here at the Greenwich Yacht Club in London's formerly industrial east end, we were close to the residue of centuries of man's efforts to tame it. Over the years the Thames has been channelled by embankment to run faster; dug out for docks; bridged and tunnelled; staircased by locks and weirs in its upper reaches; and neutered of storm surges by the Thames Barrier. Into it run its tributaries that have been buried underground as sewers, run through pipes and diverted into ponds. Today, rivers are being choked by hydroelectric dams all over the world. As I write this, the largest engineering project ever undertaken will kill nearly all China's major rivers, turning them into dead lakes and displacing around 250 million people and their history of living with and by the river.

Rivers were once the veins of the earth, providing water for drinking and agriculture and transport. Now, in London at least, the water seems an impediment, an awkward gulf that must be crossed. The rivers' glories have been its bridges and tunnels; tomorrow they will be the planned cable car crossing it in the east; one day its proudest jewel might be an airport built on an island in the estuary – so that we can fly away from it altogether! But, aside from the viewpoint of the few tourists lining the decks of the pleasure cruisers plying up and down on the brown water, it's never, these days, the river itself.

It's hard to kill a river; you can channel it or bury it but it will flow as surely as rain falls from the sky and water obeys gravity. But now I wonder how permanent even the Thames is. Nobody from London's dock days could ever have imagined the Barrier, or an island built as a terminal for jet-powered flying machines; and that leaves the future worryingly unwritten. Here in Greenwich it looks unstoppable, but perhaps if we can imagine it, one day it will happen. And if we can't imagine it, it will happen anyway – but who knows what, exactly?

In 1972 Larkin, in one of his glorious unboundings from the pressure of the landscape that surrounded him, a landscape that was constantly being bricked over before his eyes, wrote 'Chuck filth in the sea if you must: the tides will be clean beyond.' We read that at school, which was by the river, just above those tides, and somehow I knew it was true, but couldn't explain why. Years later I used to think it was a spirited *cri de coeur* from the bespectacled, porn-loving chronicler of rain and England; a generalised cry to arms for the nature that we so readily defile. But sitting by the river that day, it took on a different meaning, and I think I understood, after all those years, what he was getting at. As long as we are around, we will continue on our destructively clever paths. But the tides will outlive us, and when we are gone, they will start their slow but sure path back to their element. Maybe what Larkin was really saying is that one day we will all be dead.

While I was contemplating the end of the human race, the tide finally ran out of energy and had reached its slack low-water state before beginning its run back into town. Julian had been busy polishing off the olives and getting his head around the mess of rigging in the bottom of the boat. We stepped back in, hoisted the sail with some confusion, the two of us battling for space among the spars and mast and sailcloth and ropes, and mounted the motor in readiness – and as a legal necessity; it's illegal to go through the Thames Barrier not under power. Then we were off, under sail alone for the time being, the little Honda idling in neutral. Our circuit of the Barrier was an unnecessary extension to my circular route – a sublimely pointless journey in the first place – but the chance to sail through something so gargantuan in a boat so small was too good to pass up and I've always been in awe of the

Thames Barrier (or simply 'the Barrier' as it's known on the river).

It reminds me of a school trip to see it in the early 1980s when our teacher described it as one of the engineering marvels of the world, in a day when textbooks still, just, taught British geography in terms of what is made, or processed, where: Sheffield: steel; Manchester: textiles; Newcastle: coal. As marvels of the world go, it's more striking to me than many others like the Pyramids, because it was built out of necessity rather than vanity. The barrier is there not to trumpet civilisation, but to protect it from ruin.

It was built to protect London from storm surges in the North Sea. For a few miles each side of the river in the centre of the city, London lies on a flood plain, nowhere more than a few feet above water and sometimes below it. A big flood pouring into the tube system and flowing through the Houses of Parliament would be unthinkable. After 1928, when a flood breached the Embankment in central London, and the bigger floods of 1953, in which a storm surge in the North Sea coincided with a very high tide, killing more than 1,800 people in the Netherlands and fifty-nine on Canvey Island in the estuary, the government decided that London could never come that close again to ruin. In recent years, studies have doubted the Thames Barrier's longevity, but the latest research suggests that it is going to go the distance, protecting its city until at least 2060, by which time, if I'm still alive, I'll witness the demise of the same wonder I went to see on a school trip at the age of thirteen.

The Barrier does more than protect the city, though: to those who travel the waters of the Thames it is a dividing line between civilisation and the wilder eastern stretches of the Thames. Soon after the Barrier, the river widens further and further and, with the boggy flatlands of Essex to the north and Kent to the south, it slowly, imperceptibly changes character until it becomes a great bay and part of the North Sea – which is, in turn, part of nothing less than the Atlantic.

In the autumn of 2006, I helped bring Julian's 36-ft yacht from its summer mooring in Suffolk into London, with our mutual friend Dave and Julian's daughter Freya; a two-day trip. Until that journey into town through London's back door, I'd never realised how the city worked, how it... breathed. If the Thames is London's ancient narrative, the estuary is how the story ends. It is a dark, industrial place; a fact noted by Dickens, who made it the setting for his escaping convict, the place from where Magwitch entered the story in *Great Expectations*. In *Bleak House*, he returns to the estuary: 'It had a fearful look, so overcast and secret, creeping away so fast between the low flat lines of shore: so heavy with indistinct and awful shapes, both of substance and shadow: so deathlike and mysterious.' Joseph Conrad had a good go at describing it in *The Heart of Darkness*:

'This, also, has been one of the dark places of the earth.' He goes on to describe the lower reaches of the river as a place that appeals to the darker imagination. And it is.

Before you even get into the river from the North Sea, there are the shifting sands of the estuary to deal with: on a chart of the sea it looks like a maze. At sea, the landmarks are singular and sinister, often shrouded in mist or fog. Strange metal structures poke out of the sea in clusters, like the invaders from *War of the Worlds*. These gun emplacements were built for the war, places where men would live cooped up in close confinement for months on end, ready to train their gunsights on German bombers that hoped to pick up the reflection of the river winding through a blacked-out town, as a navigation mark to fly inland and drop bombs on the city. They shot down, between them, twenty-two German aircraft and thirteen doodlebugs, but not without human cost on the part of their operators: living in such close confinement and isolation drove the men potty, three committing suicide by 'jumping ship' and many more ending up in asylums. After the war, some of the forts were used by independent radio stations using a loophole in the law that allowed transmission from more than 3 miles offshore. In the 1960s, waves of light jazz and gangly guitar pop beamed out from these sinister rusting steel boxes atop their quadrupedal legs. Radio Essex, Screaming Lord Sutch with his Radio Sutch, Radio Invicta, King Radio and Radio City were all based on the disused platforms. In 1966, the forts would be involved in more death after a dispute erupted between Screaming Lord Sutch's manager Reg Calvert and his rival operator Major Oliver Smedley, a dispute that ended with Smedley shooting Calvert with a shotgun in self-defence. The incident and the bad, and copious, publicity that surrounded it, ushered in the end of offshore broadcasting. Since then the emplacements have been abandoned, and others were never touched again since the end of the war. It's rumoured that up there are card games in mid-hand, magazines open on pillows, half-eaten biscuits and cold cups of tea. These days, a large wind farm of great, rotating three-bladed air propellers provides a modern contrast to the old gun emplacements. On a clear day, you can see both at once. Nearby, the end of Herne Bay Pier sits decaying, cut off from land when a storm demolished it. For landsmen, piers have always been symbols born of the turn-of-the-century British obsession with sea power and expansion. To a sailor, their reason seems more apparently obvious: the pier ends provided deep-water moorings for the pleasure steamers that would take Londoners downriver on day trips to the beaches of the East Coast.

To navigate the dangerous hinterland of the estuary and get into or out of the city, you must choose a thin channel, or swatchway, and time your tides right, or you'll be aground, with potentially fatal consequences. Robin Knox-Johnston – you'll remember our determined world girdler from before, I hope – recently wrote a sailing memoir in which he rated the Thames estuary as one of the diciest places to sail.

Currents here are fast as well as murky, and that autumn we groped in the gathering dusk among the navigation buoys flashing out incomprehensible signals, as heavily built, rusting freighters chased us up the river blasting out incomprehensible, coded blasts on their deep horns. The river has its own language, unknown outside the estuary. Some of the lights flashed urgently and repeatedly to warn of danger directly to the south; others had strange, staccato rhythms and others flashed so seldom you had to stare into the darkness for a long time to check if they were really there or had just been an illusion or a drop of saltwater spray covering the eye. The whole effect was a quiet, disjointed and deadly light show to be checked hurriedly and repeatedly against the chart down in the cabin to try to make sense of it all, a task I left to Julian and Dave as I held the tiller and steered whatever course I was told to. Before complete darkness, we passed a chilling sight: the flashing lights and the radio masts of a wreck poking up above the water – but not just any wreck – this was the SS *Richard Montgomery*, a ticking time bomb.

The Americans sent her in 1944; 7,146 tons of Liberty ship, one of 2,700 of these cheap, simple ships built in a frenzy to keep up with the losses to Allied shipping in the Atlantic caused by U-boats. In the August of that year, she was loaded with a cargo of some 7,000 tons of munitions and joined a convoy bound for the UK and then on to Cherbourg in northern France. Once in the estuary, the vessel anchored off Sheerness on Kent's edge, to await the formation of a new convoy to accompany her on the next leg of the voyage across the Channel. While waiting there, the ship dragged her anchor in the shallow water and grounded on a sandbank in the middle of the Thames Estuary and at the mouth of the River Medway. The weight of the dangerous cargo broke the ship's back and these days she's a wreck, her masts (and more at low water), sticking up above the surface.

As the Receiver of Wrecks puts it: 'The vessel grounded amidships on the crest of the sandbank and intensive efforts began to unload her in order to lighten the vessel so that she could be refloated and also to save the cargo of munitions that were vital for the Allies' post-D-Day advancement. Unfortunately, by the next day, a crack appeared in the hull and the forward end began to flood. The salvage effort continued until the 25th September, by which time approximately half the cargo had been successfully removed. The salvage effort had to be abandoned when the vessel finally flooded completely.' The wreck remains there to this day, her masts still visible above the water at all states of the tide. 'There are still approximately 1,400 tons of explosives contained within the forward holds.'

Divers regularly inspect the state of the unexploded and unstable ordnance. The latest reports have hinted that it is not a question of if – just a question of when. In the sixty-odd years since her sinking the *Montgomery* has been little more than a shipping hazard, an impediment to the London Mayor Boris Johnson's plans for a grand airport in the estuary (unlike a day in a boat enjoying London's canals, I cannot help him with this), and the subject of a few sailors' jokes and a few conspiracy theories. Like why wasn't it cleared up? Is it because what's on there – illegal and undeclared biological weapons, perhaps – is so dangerous and illicit no one dares go near it? It is also a draw for tourists – different tourists – who make trips to see the ship from the water or from land on the nearby Isle of Sheppey. Whatever the truth might be, it seems likely that the SS *Richard Montgomery* will blow up one day. And bomb experts think it will be the biggest non-nuclear explosion the world has ever seen. A tsunami will rush up river and the damage will be spectacular, although, on closer inspection, most estimates reckon that the tsunami will only be 3 ft high and travel 7 miles. And the damage – some broken windows on the Isle of Sheppey.

A chilly wind blew into our faces as we struggled upriver into London against the ebbing tide, a war of attrition against a persistent head sea that slapped our speed down to just 2–3 mph under power. As the sides of the estuary drew themselves towards each other, the lights became even harder to read. In nautical iconography, a single white, solid light can mean: a boat at anchor, a craft under 7 metres long making way, or a larger craft making way seen from behind; or, in the built-up parts of the Thames Estuary, a motorcycle riding along the shore road, a house with one light on – or just about anything. Not that anyone lives here for much of our passage; large swathes of the flatlands either side of the river are as mysterious and uninhabited as they ever were in Conrad or Dickens' time. Just 30 miles upriver in the centre of London, camera-bedecked tourists consult folding street maps and cafe owners charge a lot of money for sweet, coffee-flavoured drinks with strange names. They do not know of the dark fascination that lies just outside the bright lights. We approached Queenborough on the Isle of Sheppey, well inside the 'tsunami zone', to pick up a buoy for the night. A long time ago, there was a factory here where they used to melt dead horses for glue. Julian still remembers the smell.

We tied up to an unused buoy that night and went below to our cosy bunks to listen to each other snore for a few restless hours. The next day, we passed another eerie sight – a floating pontoon over 1,000 ft long connected to the bank by jetties. Despite its size, its modest camouflage of age made it barely noticeable. But from 1930, when Tilbury Landing Stage opened, until the jet age, when it fell into disuse, this drab place and its buildings on land were the stage for the most pivotal events in many people's lives. Ashes are still scattered from this derelict site even today. It was here that people waved off relatives travelling to land far overseas, relatives they would not see for years, if ever again. It was here that the first Caribbean immigrants arrived in Britain after the war, on the *Empire Windrush* that sailed from the Caribbean to London in 1948. Most of them had no intention of staying in this cold city by the river. In 1995 the landing stage was formally reopened and these days, renamed the London Cruise Terminal, it carries on in its original capacity, much preserved: it's now once again an embarkation point for cruise ships.

Julian and I approached the Barrier in silence. The usual form is to be on the radio to Vessel Traffic Services (VST), saying something like 'VST, this is Seeker, Sierra Echo Echo Kilo Echo Romeo (or whatever your boat name is) wishing to transit the Barrier – please advise, over'. 'Seeker, this is VST – yeah, we can see you – please use the second span.' 'Copy that, fourth span, thanks VST, out.' 'Have a pleasant trip, out.'

There is something that appeals to men about speaking on the VHF radio. Firstly, because it's a privilege: you have to attend a day-course to learn to speak the lingo and use the equipment, and it's illegal to operate a VHF set without that ticket. This gives the humble VHF set the sense of something illicit, like a gun – another boon. Then there's the way it makes you speak: communication on VHF is... serious. Man stuff. It encourages a clipped form of communication about important things and brings a bit of the fighter pilot out in any sailor, even if he is dressed in yachtsman's pink trousers and has just spilled half his breakfast down his front while falling off a wave. The spelling of a boat's name in the approved phonetic alphabet (it would be unthinkable to say 'apple' and 'bertie' for A and B) is sometimes necessary; and sometimes, when the lines are clear, it's just an excuse to show how easily the operator can convert letters into things like hotels and kilos and Zulus.

The sheer occasion of speaking through this resolute, lionhearted medium has first-time users dissolve into a fit of nerves and start gabbling nonsense. In the knowledge that most channels can be heard by anyone nearby with a radio set to the same channel (other boats, harbour authorities, the Coastguard and so on), I've heard fifty-year-old company directors fall to pieces when required to ask a member of staff at a marina if he has a free berth. If the novices manage it at all, they will find the whole thing so breathlessly exciting that they will immediately forget everything they've been told and have no idea which berth number they have just been allocated. I've heard plumbers get on the radio and talk like World War Two newsreaders. With experience, the nerves dissipate, but the thrill of it lingers on in a few romantic souls, who lean against the cabins of their little yachts in lazy, priapic postures, speaking into the VHF while scanning the sea for Luftwaffe squadrons to appear on the horizon. Talking on the radio is truly one of the great little theatres of sailing.

There would be no talking on the radio today, though: I'd phoned ahead for permission to transit and we made our way quietly to the Barrier, heading for one of the enormous open gates, a large, green illuminated traffic arrow indicating that the span was in use for downstream traffic. As soon as we sailed in, our mainsail went limp and flapped around, dying in the wind shadow of the great sidewalls. The big piers the machinery stood on created strange, slow-moving eddies and great patches of oily-flat water.

It seems amazing that there are Londoners who have not stepped onto a pleasure cruiser to go and see the barrier that protects their city: it took ten years to build and spans a section of the river over a third of a mile wide. When it was opened in 1984 it was the largest moveable flood-defence barrier in the world. The Thames Barrier is the thinking man's Tower Bridge: stronger, conceptually braver, more beautiful, bigger – and a lot more necessary. Each of its four large gates is five stories high, as wide as the opening section of Tower Bridge, and tipped with a curved, glittering steel pediment reaching high above. I have sailed through Tower Bridge, its bascules raised to let me through, London's traffic brought to a standstill to let the ship pass – and it has nothing to compare to the Barrier. It is an incredible portal to a strange, powerful city.

For a few moments the boat felt slightly out of control, then we were through, the sail pulling again as we picked up pace, turned around and headed upriver through the Barrier again on the powerful flooding tide back into London, below the tall, monotonous apartment blocks built in the 1980s on the riverside when London's Docklands were regenerated. But if you want to see the rest of the Docklands, the best way is not from a boat – but from a train. Now that we no longer need our docks, we can see them for the first time from the perfect vantage point of the Docklands Light Railway that runs for miles, driverless, on elevated tracks above the old city of wharves, docks and jetties.

CHAPTER 16

THE SMALL, METALLIC TRAIN RIDE

The Docklands Light Railway. Nineteen miles, forty stations.

One of the first light rail systems in Britain, with one of the world's most advanced automatic train control systems, the DLR has expanded faster than any other UK railway.

TRANSPORT FOR LONDON

It is easy to see why some say London should never strictly be referred to as a city. In the esoteric study of urban classification, it would be better described as a 'conurbation' or a 'metropolis' – or even, more fancifully, as a 'megalopolis' or 'megaregion'. It has no defined centre: Westminster, the West End and the City are each legitimately thought of as being the bull's eye by different groups of Londoners. It was not planned; no one would ever plan a city like this – one that has grown organically in fits and spurts over many centuries. Some Londoners refer to their city as a collection of villages, though only those who live in parts of it that do resemble, and once were, villages. No one living in Stratford or Vauxhall believes himself or herself to be living the village life. And passing over the Docklands on the driverless light railway trains, you do not see village greens, brick-built post offices or thatched cottages.

Instead, an eighteenth-century civic building stands stranded on a traffic island, in a violent sea of one-way traffic swirling all around. An old church spire sticks up above a Georgian pub, long-disused, the two ring-fenced by a perimeter of 1960s-built tower blocks. By the river are the endless banks of flats, all pale brick, glass and steel, and all 'luxury'. The elevated Docklands Light Railway runs above it all, straightlining over the endless convulsions of Bow Creek below it, then diving under the river to emerge alongside more inlets and docks. Warehouses old and new are here and there and always, above the whole mess, are the skyscrapers of commerce – or, these days, of fear. A riveted iron Victorian bridge curves over a road, both disused. Perhaps it was built to cross some stream that has since been paved over and culverted from sight below ground. Flyovers, in the deathly hue of concrete, echo with the endless hollow boom of their traffic. Building sites stand next to empty pitches of gravel, some surrounded by crabby grass, some fenced with chain-link steel wearing crowns of barbed wire or its nastier brother, razor wire.

There's the Dome; half an onion upside down with knitting needles jabbed into it, a twentieth-century folly that eventually found its calling as a venue for pop music: saved by its capacity for profit and popular taste, it has become a church to the Gods of money and vanity, a church whose congregation is greater and noisier than any real one. Other buildings are inexplicable: a funnel rising out of a low, concrete bunker with a locked door at one end. The flats on the riverside have glassed-in balconies bearing cold-looking stainless-steel table-and-chair sets. *You should see the view*, their owners maintain. On a summer's night, it would be exciting, the glitter of water, the rushing of trains, the sounds of the city's heart pumping blood around its arteries carrying for miles in the warm air. In the day, it must look decrepit and monotonous. Car parks, gas storers, the sort of big electric pylons that carry power lines by motorways but should never be seen in cities; graffiti, building cranes, bus depots. In this ugly pandemonium, you never know what you will see next. The Docklands are repulsive, slightly sinister – hellish and Ballardian in turns – and exciting. They are London's hallway. They are where you dump the necessities – coats and umbrellas – before you proceed to the inner calm of the sitting room. Portakabins here, and over there, a row of perfectly ordinary, post-war suburban-style houses in dark red brick. Dock buildings flash by, then docks themselves, these days prettified and soulless in the main, our maritime past turned into a series of ornamental ponds for the enjoyment of listless city workers eating their sandwiches at lunchtime as they peer into the depths of their smartphones; it's not the worst fate for old docks, by any means. Further east is the ExCel Centre, an exhibition centre as big as a small town, surrounded by the old black cranes that used to unload ships in the days before containerisation. They have been painted jet black and look predatory, as stylised as any carnivorous insect or plant from an old disaster movie.

South of the Thames, trains run above Deptford Creek, where another of London's tidal rivers, the Ravensbourne, ends its 11-mile journey through the green lands of south London to be flushed out into the mudbanks of the Thames, running over a little step to form a weir. There used to be mills here and, in the twentieth century, yet another hulking power station. They used to build warships here, for three centuries from the 1500s. Now, a couple of old, wooden workboats nestle into the mud as the river trickles out at low tide, baulked against the metal pilings that have hemmed the river in. The buildings here, near Lewisham, are eccentric, layer upon layer of time peeled away. Old warehouses lie behind the boats, intriguingly unrestored, hanging onto time, biding their days until the powers that be get their next big idea and tear them down. Under the elevated railway tracks lies a crowded little encampment of caravans, clustering to the bridge supports like mussels to a rope.

And the old workboats, both dark blue, are clearly live-aboards. I wonder if this is a paid-for mooring. It seems impossible that anyone has counted this little section of river, that anyone could care about it. Which, if it's true, can only be a good thing for the inhabitants of these two boats, because in England, caring about a thing is almost always a prerequisite for demanding profit from it. They sit there, still with the buoyant, pugnacious little bodies that speak of stronger days. River tugs perhaps, or cargo boats – but real seagoing boats, retired up an ugly creek under a railway track. If they were men, and boats are not, contrary to tradition, all female – some are clearly men – they would be retired fishermen or boatbuilders in the corner of a waterside pub, gazing out at the empty docks that have been turned into yacht marinas for London types down for the weekend, slowly sinking pint after pint of bitter. Slow, deliberate, calm and content. Good men, but slow to smile – and hard to get to know, their faces as elusive and deeply wrinkled as the paintwork on these two old boys under the railway, cracking away from the hulls in layers, a rich study in the texture of neglect.

A huge, colourful graffito above, in the angular, 3D high-colour style of the 1980s, read 'GetUpAndPanik'. It might as well have been for people like me, entranced by the views out of the window, who have just realised they're about to miss their stop.

CHAPTER 17
SAILING ON SKIN

Thames Barrier to Greenwich. Two
miles. The Isle of Dogs, sailing over
subterranea and London's lost rivers.

*Tread carefully over the pavements of
London for you are treading on skin.*

PETER ACKROYD

The Isle of Dogs is not an island at all, but a teardrop
peninsula of the north bank that the Thames would,
if left to its own devices, eventually cut through and leave
behind as an oxbow lake. These days it's home to the great
skyscrapers of high finance, but it's probably most famous
of all for its daily TV appearance as the star of the opening
credits of EastEnders, these days coloured in a rather
optimistic Mediterranean blue.

What hasn't changed is how long it takes to get around
it. In the days of sail, it made the route as indirect as
a horseshoe, with the power to cause great delays and

frustration to vessels trying to sail into or out of central London. The problem was, and still is, that there is no favourable wind to get a sailor round, as the permutation of directions it takes on its course means that even a constant wind will hit the sails at different angles as a boat makes its way around. And there is the more simple reason that it adds a lot of distance to the journey. Julian and I were lucky that day, reaching across a following breeze, the wind behind us again as we went down one side of the U shape then reaching up the other side as the wind veered around the clock to ease us on our way. Soon we were past the Isle of Dogs and running west again, the wind still, miraculously, at our backs. The tide was with us too, increasing in force all the time. It made for calm, fast conditions and we flew into town on the brown water, the sun glinting off the glass and steel lining the banks of the river.

By the time we'd reached Tower Bridge, the Thames had already been crossed by more than a dozen tunnels invisible under our keel, from the Channel Tunnel Rail Link under the estuary to the Greenwich Foot Tunnel on the south side of the river, which we sailed over now. Its handsome, glazed entry dome, which glows a rich, deep yellow at night, sits just below the *Cutty Sark*, the famous clipper ship kept on land by the river, Britain's only ship recorded as a Grade 1 listed building, the surest guarantee that she will never return to her saltwater element. Not so *Gipsy Moth IV* that used to sit in another concrete depression beside her, rotting under the rain that is wooden boats' biggest enemy and a regular recipient of the hard knocks of teenage vandalism. She was put there in 1967 after her sixty-five-year-old daredevil skipper Sir Francis Chichester sailed her around the world solo, south of the great capes, ostensibly in an effort to beat the times set by clippers like the *Cutty Sark*. He stopped only once, in Australia.

He never managed to beat the clipper ships' old records, but he did become a national hero. If the reports of the time are to be trusted, half a million people arrived to see the nerdy-looking bespectacled hero sail back into Portsmouth on his strange ketch that looked like something out of *Thunderbirds*. It was after his return that sailors like Robin Knox-Johnston realised the only big navigational prize left to sailors was to circumnavigate the globe without stopping at all. Chichester hated *Gipsy Moth IV*, though – he called her his 'cantankerous ketch' and was happy enough to see her dumped on land, never to sail again.

When she was fished out of her bunker and restored to go around the world again by the sailing magazine *Yachting Monthly* in 2006, seemingly every journalist in the land had a go holding the tiller, going out for short joyrides in the Solent. The yacht's skipper, Richard Baggett, who could roll a cigarette one-handed while sailing into a Force 5, became quite used to these joyrides for novices: the BBC, Radio 4, ITV and Channel 5 all wanted to have a go holding the long, extravagantly curved wooden tiller. I joined the boat for a two-day passage from Plymouth to the Isle of Wight, her final resting place, and ran her straight over a lobster pot while at the helm. The engine made a hideous choking, clattering noise as though jumping up and down to escape its mounts, and long moments of damage assessment passed, during which I thought I'd broken a national treasure, but a dive overboard with a bread knife by the skipper had us going again soon enough.

The Greenwich Foot Tunnel was opened in 1902. It's 1,217 ft long and, until very recently, it had a manned lift. A man of indeterminate character, and seemingly as old as the tunnel itself, ran it up and down on its endless two-way journey. Perhaps he wasn't real at all, but a ghost. The tunnel, like the Woolwich tunnel nearby, is being refurbished and perhaps the lift won't be manned in the future. But in the foot tunnel itself, which is always empty in my memory, you will still be able to hear the short echo of the concrete tunnel, that urban reverb sound from a hundred films, the sound that is heard by the sinister man following. I am confident that if you ever decide you would like to be murdered traditionally, and with some old-London romance to it, this will still be an excellent place to come.

London is probably the most tunnelled city in the world, for the simple reason that it is built on a substratum of clay, unlike, for instance, New York; I say 'probably', as many tunnels are secret and do not appear on maps. Manhattan Island is built on rock with names like schist and gneiss, names that sound as tough as Vikings, names as tough as the reputation of its inhabitants; so while it provided a good anchor for skyscrapers, London's 'quoggy' ground provided an ideal habitat for tunnelling surreptitiously like moles.

Serious tunnelling started in the nineteenth century for the tube network, and back then Britain was still a Christian nation whose people feared the consequences of burrowing into the territory of the devil. A journalist of the time went to see one of the first new underground trains pull in to a station and described the noise of its approach as 'the screaming of 10,000 demons', which is exactly the sound they still make today if you are open to such dramatic interpretation. Before that, though, many of the city's rivers were being buried, although there are few that don't make their presence felt here and there, either in person, or by the street names that remember them on the surface above. They live on in people's fears too: most reports of ghosts are found above or very near the courses of buried rivers, and it's probably the gushing sounds of water underneath buildings that produce noises like the rustling of skirts and petticoats.

Most subjects, however arcane-seeming, have their great chroniclers. In the case of London's lost rivers, the one-book canon belongs to a man named Nicholas Barton, whose exhaustive tome *The Lost Rivers of London* bears all the patient research of the meticulous local historian, which is what he was.

From this book, I learned that a little footbridge I had passed under back on the Regent's Canal carried the River

Tyburn under pedestrians' feet. There is no clue of it apart from a few metal inspection hatches laid into the pavement of the bridge. In Regent's Park it was dammed to form a boating lake, where forty people drowned after skating its thin ice in 1867. These days a tributary of it runs in a conduit barely two foot wide through the bottom of a covered market, Gray's Antiques, who found it running through their basement while doing building work in 1977. They've preserved their bit and it's now an ornament of the shop, complete with a small footbridge and goldfish. It must be their best find. The Tyburn's outfall, under a house built over the river, was a place I'd seen for years while canoeing – it's very near my club in Pimlico. 'Must be a sewer,' someone said, and that was the end of it at the time. You don't have to go on the river to see the Tyburn, though... thousands of Londoners see it every day as they wait on the platform at the world's oldest underground station, Baker Street, built in 1863. Here it runs in a white-painted iron pipe over the Circle Line and Hammersmith and City Line platforms, just as the Westbourne does over the District Line at Sloane Square.

The Fleet is London's best-known 'other river'. Its two main sources run across Hampstead Heath, the high hilly park in the north of the city. It can be seen; in fact, thousands bathe in it every summer when they swim in the heath's popular ponds. It is then demoted to subterranean sewers; broad, oval avenues, high enough for a man to walk in (and the sewermen do), that carry it down to the Thames where it enters the river at Victoria Embankment under Blackfriars

Bridge. Apparently you can hear it outside The Coach and Horses pub on Ray Street. I went there once, after weeks of dry weather, and lay down in the middle of the road outside the pub, ear pressed to a cold metal drainage grate, keenly aware of the eyes of passing pedestrians. Even without recent rain, I could hear it gushing by at speed with a stronger voice than most country brooks. Clearly, the Fleet was once a river of grandeur.

The rivers live on in a sense: a plaque here, a street name there; a winding street that once followed its meanders down to the river; a boating or a swimming lake; a hinged iron door let into the embankment of the river, belching water out in heavy rainfall when the tide on the Thames is low.

Today, they are being rediscovered by a select few: urban explorers, who trespass on hidden corners of the city to take photographs. Theirs is an illegal and dangerous calling. To anyone but each other, they are anonymous as they infiltrate the past – the old rivers and sewers, disused underground stations, the tops of condemned buildings – and the future; buildings still in build. These are people who love the undisturbed decay of age. One of them writes on his website: 'Unbelievable stories always happen in the past, in the future or parallel universes.'

After I wrote up the story of my trip in London's listings magazine, *Time Out*, I received a few complaints from loyal south Londoners, claiming that I'd only been around north London. To a tourist, the city north of the river *is* London – or at least most of it. There are beautiful parts of south London and although most of the city's main attractions – the West End, the City, Westminster, Trafalgar Square, St Paul's Cathedral and so on – are north of this arbitrary divide, I'd actually seen most of south London's famous sites too as they are ranged along the river's edge: the Southbank Centre, including the Royal Festival Hall, the Millennium Wheel and historic Greenwich. But there are strong divisions in London – east versus west and north versus south. The north/south divide can run strong. It is a dull, didactic exchange in which the same lines are trotted out by each side, and it doesn't seem as though anyone really cares who wins. According to south Londoners, north London is full of pretentious, dull-eyed plutocrats with no sense of community, four-wheel-drive 'Chelsea tractors' and children with names like Arabella and Horatio. According to north Londoners, south London is an endless, incomprehensible wasteland of crab grass and council flats, a failed suburbia where you can score crack more easily than hail a taxi.

There is only a small element of truth on either side; in reality, both Londons exist on both sides of the river. The real reason I'd not sailed around the entirety of London's massive conurbation of 13 million souls and 3,300 square miles was only that it cannot be done – there is no loop that takes in a decent chunk of the city south of the Thames, but that is not to say the southern half is without its rivers and canals. And it did rankle a bit that I'd not seen any of them. A year after completing my journey, I quelled a long-harboured curiosity and headed to Wimbledon to navigate a river that runs through the south of the city. I'd always heard it could be done, but had only previously experienced it in small parts.

CHAPTER 18

BURIED ALIVE

South Wimbledon to Wandsworth on the River Wandle. Five miles, thirty bridges. Canoeing down south London's unknown jewel.

Of all London's rivers, [the River Wandle]
particularly seems to resent being buried alive.

ORMSBY, C/O NICHOLAS BARTON

The River Wandle, unlike the tidal Thames, *is* the sort of river beloved by poets. It might have been constrained, distorted and tamed by concrete banks, steel sides, shallow weirs and width constraints where it flows through bridge spans and under buildings, but still it tumbles and tinkles, and the water is clear enough to see the weeds streaming out underneath as they follow the river's flow. Or it would be the sort of river beloved by poets if it didn't have the wastelands of south London crowding up to the edge.

The Wandle is only navigable by the most versatile and ancient craft of them all, so I loaded the roof rack of the car with a bright-orange, plastic kayak and, after driving across London north to south, arrived at the river's edge below a cuboid shopping complex. The Wandle was low, but flowing swiftly past, raising little trains of waves, and the stirring of it caused it to release its ancient scent – the timeless, rotten smell that speaks of millennia of decomposition – the familiar smell of my childhood and the same smell as the Thames. I put on, snapping the spraydeck over the cockpit and sliding over the pebbles into the flow, which was about six inches deep, and, instantly, the little boat and I were swept away. Even this miniature waterway poses all the same problems as bigger rivers. At low water, you are forever scraping over stones and getting stuck. High water presents its own dangers – in this case getting stuck under a low bridge or pipe as the water rises to meet it, a situation that could easily end up in drowning. At this level, the river is safe, although the bridges are low enough that I had to duck while going under some of them.

We took a sharp left and started to drift alongside a wooded park, thick with graffiti, branches fallen from trees and even a deserted pram. There was no need to paddle, apart from the odd corrective stroke to keep the boat on course. This was the free ride, the perfect sightseeing river that moves fast enough to simply drift. For a while, I kept pace with a jogger on the towpath who looked extremely surprised to see a boat drifting past alongside him. Unlike the canals and the river, which are full of boats, the Wandle is simply too urban, too shallow, and not well enough known to attract many boats. Even among canoeists (and canoes are the only craft that can navigate waters like this), it falls between two camps: too urban, too ugly and not nearly challenging enough for a serious white-water practitioner, and slightly too tricky for a complete beginner. Besides, it is hardly known, even in London.

Later, I overtook a familiar figure, a representative of a strange, small niche that one sees from time to time in the city: the bandy-legged pensioner, baseball cap pulled onto his head, speed-walking, with an aggressive, jerking gait. If he was surprised, he didn't show it – perhaps he'd seen most things in his long experience, or perhaps he just didn't care any more. Later, we passed the obligatory dog walker and three boys in a playing field wearing school uniform, smoking cigarettes and watching the little orange kayak and its paddler go by with blank expressions. One of them spat on the ground and rubbed it in with his trainer. *Like I give a fuck...*

The most common actors from London's cast of extras who people the green spaces and watersides were the young women pushing prams, desperate for any new route that relieves the tedium of pushing baby around for hours on end. *It's the only way he'll sleep,* they will complain to others of their tribe when they meet at their watering holes for cappuccinos.

The river sped up into a curling white recirculating wave as it narrowed under an old mill building. A recirculator traps floating objects, like branches, rubbish and canoeists, and spins them around for a while before spitting them out downstream. Some, known as keepers, never throw the object far enough into the down flow, and then canoeists drown, spinning endlessly in the vortex. This vortex is known as a 'stopper' or 'pourover', and occurs when a sudden dip in level causes the accelerating water to dig a hole for itself, the water immediately downstream falling back in on the surface, the main flow carrying on underneath. This was a small one, and I took a few paddle strokes and burst through it easily, emerging the other side of the mill building, now private residences. A plaque on its side stated that the building, in itself 200 years old, stands on a site where milling had been carried out for 700 years, and the power of the water, created by narrowing the little river, is still there.

Later, the towpath disappeared and we were alone, floating past the back of an electricity substation and a large repository of skips stacked one on top of the other. The backs of ageing warehouses with mono-pitched roofs come right down to the water's edge, with extensions added over the years leaning this way and that, and outside, piles of oil drums and a small fire burning in an old steel hospital trolley, sending tentacles of smoke up into the still, dry air. An unlikely looking character was tending to the fire, a thin, middle-aged man in trainers and tracksuit trousers, a smart blue blazer and a head of hair that looked like a solid grey wave breaking at sea. Apart from him that side of the river was deserted.

Further on, there were thickets of trees, and behind them the sounds of birds mingled with the beeps of a lorry backing up with a happy robotic chant – 'Attention, the vehicle is reversing.' A strip of allotments slid past us, potting sheds at the back rambling down to the water's edge. Here and there, in warehouse car parks, were old buses laid up to end their days. Canalsides and roadsides like this attract old buses. They come singly and in pairs, whole fleets dispersed to die, scattered throughout the sidings of the city. The walker's path running alongside the river for most of its route was lined with the obligatory props of the urban waterway: an unused kayak lying upside down in weeds – an old GRP Gaybo Olymp IV, I noticed, as I used to paddle one; blackberry bushes below jetliner vapour trails; the odd bench with its ring of spent lager cans, white plastic bags and plastic bottles, their identifying labels washed off by the water; wooden doors that had passed their best: perhaps the owners had gone for the more modern 'open look', knocking sitting rooms into kitchens, in the domestic version of era-shock... *We wanted to keep the outside original and create a clean, modern space inside...*

Styrofoam cups lay cushioned in nettles. Plastic was invented on the banks of a river and it has wanted to return ever since. Blankets of creeping weeds climbed the trunks of dead trees. Nearby, the appalled gaze of a bearded man rendered in spray can looked down from a stranded brick wall. It took me a second to realise that it was the King of

Hearts, presiding over a small cluster of veal-yellow fast-food containers at his feet.

I was wet by now, the constant waves of the river slowly soaking into my neoprene spraydeck and down towards my feet. The inside of a kayak is never dry, the hollow shell always running with puddles from its last expedition. On this trip, the water soaking into me from the bottom upwards was the Atlantic, a remnant of a surfing trip off the north Cornish coast.

Long concrete cills were appearing in the river now, running down the middle and I steered one side of them, then the other. The 5 miles from south Wimbledon had flown by with the little river pushing me along as fast as a Lycra-clad jogger in late middle age.

We flew past a storage centre with a small pile of rusting sea containers on one side and, behind the breeze-block, razor-wire-topped wall, the tip of the mast of a stranded yacht. The first signs of the approaching Thames had started to appear. The banks, free earlier, were now hemmed in by concrete and steel pilings as the river marshalled its forces for the final run-out. The robin redbreasts had been replaced by groups of seagulls, stuck in their own tragedy of relocation; they chased each other's tails and cawed hungrily, majestic birds circling the river, eyes hunting... for edible rubbish and half-eaten hamburgers.

I was so taken by the undignified compromises that seagulls have to make in their new urban habitat that the Southside Shopping Centre crept up on me quickly and, before I could take stock of it, I was swept into the square black hole underneath it. I discovered a rushing darkness, with the weight of shops, cinemas, shoplifting teenagers and buggies and prams all seemingly pressing down on my head. A moment of fear passed through me, making me feel queasy. Unlike the canals or the Thames, this waterway was never meant to be used. A minute or two and 400 metres later, I was in the cold, sunny air again, pale-blue sky above, passing the Young's brewery and making my final run-out to the Thames. At the mouth of the creek in Wandsworth I joined London's main river again and went west a few yards until I found a jetty and, kayak on shoulder, walked up to the embankment, hiding the boat and wandering off, an unlikely figure in a crash helmet and drysuit, and a spraydeck hanging down to my knees, appearing something like an astronaut who'd lost his suit and clothed himself in an old tarpaulin.

The Thames had one last surprise for me that day. I thought I'd seen it in every mood, but that day, the high pressure that had made the day so bright had flattened the river into a mirror. Not a boat was in sight and the reflection of the sky was perfect, turning the river blue, with clouds scudding across its surface. A V-formation of starlings flew over and looked like fish swimming through clouds under the surface. A pair of eights went skimming past and the reflections bent out of shape then disappeared. Even Wandsworth Bridge, which normally looks like something found in a charity shop compared to its glamorous brothers, like Albert Bridge and Tower Bridge, was doing its best to make the most of its shabby-chic charm. I trudged around the waterfront for a bit, looking at the cold building faces and pedestrianised alleys, complete with anti-parking bollards, which led to the blocks of flats. Behind them, whole shopping streets were boarded up, awaiting demolition to make way for more new monoliths.

Everywhere there is water these days, streets and old houses like these are being swept away by the relentless tide of glass and steel. The haberdasher, the family butcher, the shop that used to sell remote-controlled cars and models and the bookshop, have all had to make way for it; a collection of deceased shopfronts of humanity bowing before the new buildings. And that day, it seemed somehow as though our interests have become so very few. Where once there were so many things, so many nooks, crannies, shops and hobbies, now there is only high-speed Internet, 'pampering', mini-breaks, luxury windowless shower-rooms appended to every room, pink paving, anti-parking bollards, restrictions on movement and locked gates denying access to the river in labyrinthine mazes. If you can still get down to the river in the centre of London, you'll be among the quiet cameras on their tall metal poles, always watching. It seemed that day as though it were the buildings themselves, with their cold, hateful architecture, that accepted the mediocrity, celebrated the expenditure, and bred the violence recorded by those monstrous eyes on stalks. Next door to it all was an oasis – an old riverside pub; a warm, stubborn relic. It was time for a solitary pint on the veranda, as the sun started to drop away upriver.

CHAPTER 19

DOWNTOWN

Greenwich to Hungerford Bridge. Six
miles, nine bridges. The brownness of
the river and the secrets it hides.

*In the River Thames, in an Arctic iceberg, in your
drinking glass, in that drop of rain, on that frosty
window pane, in your eyes, in every other microscopic
part of you (and me), all waters converge.*

RONI HORN

Back on the Thames, Julian and I were making good
progress, a little green dot on a sea of brown. The
brownness of the Thames is something that has captivated
anyone who has studied it long enough: one of the river's
many nicknames down the years has been 'the brown
goddess'. It is the richest, densest brown imaginable, like
(cold) hot chocolate and, although, on closer inspection, the
colour is suspended in particles, it looks as though the entire
river has been coloured with a powerful dye. Divers measure
visibility underwater in metres: ten and under is considered

ropey, 15 metres is considered good-ish, 50 metres the dive of a lifetime. The visibility in the Thames is about 30 cm. The river is like a blanket. There is no technology yet invented that can see through it. Sonar will bounce echoes off the bottom to render its form on a computer screen; but it remains that nothing can actually see what's on the bottom of that river. If you want to see anything under the waters of the Thames, you have to get in there and drag it out from her embrace. The artist Roni Horn recently staged an exhibition of her brilliant close-up textural photos of the river in the Tate Modern on the banks of the Thames – yet another disused power station in fact – and posed the question: what is that stuff flowing outside the window? It's not water, surely? Water is a clear, colourless, odourless, tasteless liquid. The Thames is none of those things.

It is a well-documented fact that the Thames, in its days of heaviest use, was biologically dead; nothing lived in it. And it's an equally well-documented fact that it's now one of the cleanest rivers in the industrialised world, full of all sorts of life, from seals and otters to breeding populations of cod and even the odd seahorse and other exotic visitors as the seas of the world grow warmer. Once I came out of St Katharine Docks near Tower Bridge on a motorboat owned by a keen Kiwi fisherman. Almost all boats above the size of a dinghy carry an echo sounder; they pre-date the ubiquitous satnav by decades, based as they are on the sonar developed by the Allies in World War Two to pinpoint the menace of U-boats under the waves.

Their purpose these days is to tell you how much water you have under your keel and in some parts of our coast, they must be watched with a hawk's eyes: the numbers flicker up and down and when they get uncomfortably close to a grounding, you tack and turn, sailing away into deeper water. It's a law that this vital instrument will always be placed just behind the only place in the cockpit left to sit down and the moment you do sit down, the skipper will bark at you to move, as he can't see his echo sounder any more. This Kiwi's echo sounder was a more sophisticated version and acted as a fish-finder as well, showing shoals of fish where it picked them up under the keel, and as soon as he turned it on, it was alive with little pixellated fish swimming along below our boat. I assumed that the echo sounder was picking up on sediment in the water and bouncing false echoes back, the same way that the screen of a radar detector fills up with 'clutter' at sea, and I put the theory to the Kiwi, who seemed amazed by the question.

'What are they?! They're fish, mate,' he replied, astonished, then went on to explain that his fish-finder didn't report clutter – there had to be something down there. If there was – and to this day, I find it difficult to believe – the idea of fish born to that blanket of filth was an unsettling one.

Everyone wants a superpower. As children we dream of flight, invisibility, teleportation, extraordinary strength, ESP... I dreamed of the ability to teleport and become invisible as much as everyone else. But there was another superpower I always dreamed of as well: the ability to sprinkle magic dust on the river and make it transparent. It was a thrilling idea, but also a frightening one. What is down there is a secret that to this day nobody knows. We know how deep it is; the tidal sections have been thoroughly charted for depth and underwater obstructions, just as they have been at sea. We know the character of the bottom; mud here, sand there, chalk in the estuary and sometimes broken shell. And we know the temperature of the water, the speed and direction of its tidal currents and the rise and fall of its tides. We have a rough idea of what's living in there from catches in the estuary and a thousand audit projects carried out over the years.

But one summer's day in 2005, a journalist from *Angler's Mail* was tramping the foreshore just behind the office, a large tower built by the Thames, and saw a dead sturgeon floating past. Until that day it was thought they were extinct on the London River: it was the first seen there for nearly 150 years. Consider the men with metal detectors and sharp eyes who can be seen on any of the river's London beaches when the tide is down; do they ever find anything? Every time they go, almost. Pottery, like pipes, from as early as the thirteenth century is so common it's barely worth picking up. Shipwrecks, buried just below the mud and shingle, turn up with surprising regularity as well. A recent audit of wrecks on the bottom of the river and its estuary by the Port of London Authority and

Wessex Archaeology made surprising reading. How many would you guess? Fifty? Maybe a hundred? Of known wrecks, there are 1,100. How many others are down there defies any guessing.

Floating down a transparent Thames might be something like flying over an alien landscape of wrecks, ancient detritus and giant fish floating in the ether. Of course, this mystery applies to most large bodies of water – the sea more than anywhere. But to think that there is something undiscovered running through the centre of London is more surprising. I need to remind myself constantly that the river is – by far – the oldest thing in the city.

There hadn't been much else on the river in east London, jut the odd clipper boat, and the commuter catamarans that ply their trade from the east into the centre of town, zipping by smoothly and quietly at over twenty knots, leaving a wash that, imperceptible on the river, circulates deep and erodes the mud covering the shingle of the foreshore. Those, and a rigid inflatable boatful of Secret Boat Service men clad in black – we will return to them later.

From 1690, the world's first submarine was busy on trials on this stretch of the Thames. Built by Cornelius van Drebbel, a Dutchman serving in the British Royal Navy, it was formed of oiled leather stretched over a wooden frame. In a contemporary painting, it looks like a greasy, leather catfish swimming just below the surface, propelled by oarsmen sitting inside. It travelled at between 12 and 15 ft below the surface and could apparently stay under for three hours, enough to travel from Westminster to Greenwich.

Early afternoon on that long day, we sailed under Tower Bridge: as we drew into town, the second-oldest thing in London was enjoying his turn at the helm and the river was filled with pleasure cruisers, their washes and voices bouncing back and forth across the river between the built-up embankments. We'd hear snatches of tannoy, like 'We are now passing the Monument, built in the late seventeenth century to commemorate the Great Fire of London.' A few moments later, their wash would hit us, sending the little Storm pitching up and down in the waves. 'Looking rather shiny, isn't it?' asked Julian with a wry smile as we passed said Monument. 'One of yours?' I asked. He nodded. When not sailing, Julian is a restoration architect and works on amazing buildings like the disused aircraft hangars and industrial edifices he has a great admiration for – as well as famous landmarks like the Monument. The top was aflame in new gold leaf and it looked, to my layman's eye, as though he'd shined it up a treat, and I was glad I'd just heard the tannoy from the pleasure cruiser, because in truth, I don't know what half of London's landmarks are and until that moment I had no idea what the Monument was; and that would never have done in front of Julian. The Monument is one of London's earliest landmarks, built in 1667 to commemorate the passing of the Great Fire and as a symbol of optimism for the future. In eighteenth-century paintings of London's river by Canaletto, only the Monument and St Paul's Cathedral remain the same. Even the river looks different – wider, and filled with hundreds of watermen ferrying passengers from one side to the other.

Moments later, invisible from our level, we passed a statue to a certain engineer called Isambard Kingdom Brunel. The river was getting bouncier, the bridges lower, and we put the sail away. In the distance, we could see the angular, spindly form of the Hungerford Bridge.

CHAPTER 20

A TALE OF TWO SHIPS

Hungerford Bridge to Pimlico
on the River Thames. One and a
half miles, three bridges. The
Marchioness, an earlier disaster,
the evacuation of Dunkirk and
a familiar riverside haunt.

*The disco was coming alive with people singing
to the Hues Corporation. Rock the boat, don't tip
the boat over, they yelled. Unbelievable, but true.*

MAGDA ALLANI, *MARCHIONESS* SURVIVOR.

The night of 19 August 1989 was a perfect late-summer London night; the sort when the sky is the clearest, darkest, most electric blue and the river, a perfectly black mirror, is so still it reflects each individual window pane from the Houses of Parliament above. Sound, much of it laughter, travels more clearly and, seen from the south bank,

Big Ben is pin-sharp, appearing nearer in the clear air, its top glowing emerald green.

In the air that night, a full astronomer's moon floated above, the waters of the planet's northern hemisphere bulging towards its pull. A closer look at the river would have shown it rushing into London at 3 knots, a brisk walking pace, swirling around bridge stanchions and creating slack backwatering eddies as it rounded corners.

For six hours, twice a day, the North Sea forces its way upriver into London. In the Thames Estuary, a rising tide pools out slowly over the mudflats of Essex and Kent. The entire landscape is transformed into a new shape. Land disappears. Mud is covered and water comes all the way to the grassy shores. Boats resting on the mud start to shift about, imperceptibly at first, then float. Other yachts, in deeper water and already afloat tied to mooring buoys, start swinging around to face the opposite direction. Boats are shaped like fish and will move on their own to feel the water's flow parting at their noses and flowing down their flanks. Jetties start to creak, then rise up on the water, the angle of the gangways connecting them to land becoming gentler. People who live on barges will be able to walk up and down them easily rather than take on the hike that they present at low tide. Later, as the sea reaches the city, it will pick up some of the city's colour on its face: it will turn browner as it mixes with London's ancient sediment and becomes river.

By about Westminster, the river will be undecided if it's still the sea or has become the river, having been tamed and defiled by the stink of the city. On an ebbing tide it will taste of metal and rotting vegetation. Now, on our flood tide, it will have a tang of salt. On its surface it will bear marks from its journey; bits of rubbish it dislodged from the beaches as they disappeared under it: driftwood, sculpted into Barbara Hepworth curves; leaves that dropped gently from the branches of the grand old oak trees overhanging the Embankment in Pimlico; little floating islands of plastic bottles and crisp packets, swirling on the surface as they move into town. The river is moving outward, covering the banks and doubling its surface area; it is moving upwards, halving the 'air draught' – the height between the water's surface and the bottom of the London bridges. And it is moving up the river, between the banks and into the land. In every possible way, the tide comes in as slowly and invisibly as an hour hand and as surely as its powerful alibi: time itself.

That summer of 1989, I was on the Thames canoeing nearly every day, with my friends from the club. The warm, long summer holidays were a perfect chance to practise stability manoeuvres like righting a destabilised kayak with high and low braces; darting in and out of the pumping flow of the power station wave at Lots Road Power Station; climbing up the wooden mooring posts, called 'dolphins', that used to stick out of the river near Grosvenor Road, hauling our boats behind us, balancing on the top, snapping on spraydecks and dropping into the river in a manoeuvre known as a 'seal launch'. We were also learning the vital arts of soaking each other in splash fights, jumping off the bridges into the river and, at low water, sometimes just beaching up outside the comical building in Vauxhall that houses MI6 (one of central London's best beaches) and watching the river go by, feet in the water, and wading in for the occasional swim in that hot, long summer of my childhood. Behind us, a buried iron gate set into the river wall let the buried River Effra escape into the Thames.

For my friends and me at the Westminster Boating Base, it was our second full summer of paddling; we'd continued every week throughout the winter, too, becoming so cold that afterwards, back at the club and in the hot showers, our entire bodies would sting like nettle rash as blood returned to dead limbs. It felt like an exquisite, healing sort of poison.

We paddled long, heavy kayaks called Mirages. They were among the first plastic kayaks built (if you can call melting in a spinning oven 'building'). The Mirage, for those who don't know it, bears no similarity to the beautiful French fighter jets built by Dassault, which share the name, and used to scream over the French lake when I was younger. It was, and is, an ugly, unwieldy craft that probably put quite a few young canoeists off the sport for good. The ones we used at our club were once white but the river had quickly turned them the colour of dirty laundry. They rose out of the water slightly at bow and stern, giving them the foolish cheerfulness of a smiling croissant; a croissant that, with its tiny cockpit, would entrap you and try to drown you the minute you capsized. In the summer of 1989, we had yet to learn the crux manoeuvre, the Eskimo roll that brings the paddler and boat back upright with a sweep of the paddle – although we spent a lot of time perfecting the first half of that manoeuvre.

We knew basic river craft, though... we'd learned to hug the shore when paddling against the tide, where the current is weakest. A kayak can float in four inches of water and can make way against the tide not by brute force but by complete oneness with its environment, tucking in tight and making the minutest course adjustments, second by second, inch by inch, to use every micro eddy and current. We learned to keep clear of fixed objects in moving water; even a slight current, unnoticeable when you are flowing with it, can pin floating objects with tons of pressure against static objects. We were particularly warned about the moored steel lighters, great unpowered barges that used to unload the ships in the Pool of London before containerisation and ships with deeper draughts ended the lighters and lightermen and shut down London as a working port. Their prows were slanted and, once sucked under them, you'd be pinned, flushed from your boat and eventually emerge the other end. Only half the small number of people who've made that swim have survived.

We learned to stick to the correct, right, side of the river and to approach fixed objects like our embarking and disembarking pontoon, against the tide, and under control. We also learned which boats gave the biggest wash, which we'd try to surf, and how waves jacked up and grew in size when they started shelving in the shallows of the muddy beaches. We were learning the dangers of our new environment. But more than that, we were learning the pleasures of our new, magnificent playground.

That night, 19 August, the pressure was high, meaning the weight of the sky above was pushing down on the rivers and seas, leavening the waves and soothing their vigour. One hundred and thirty-one people also about to treat the Thames as their playground were boarding a small, steel river cruiser called the *Marchioness*, just 86 ft long. She was built in 1923 and her hull was slender and elegant, but no layman would ever notice this under her high, boxy superstructure ringed by large, square picture windows all the way around. Adapted to cruise the placid Thames as a party boat, her demeanour was as friendly and tubby as Thomas the Tank Engine. In those days, we used to pass the *Marchioness* often as she plied up and down. I knew many of the boats of the river in those days, and made a note of remembering their names. The *Marchioness* and the *Hurlingham*, a similar boat, were among the busiest and we'd see them all the time.

Unlike little unpowered dinghies, such as my Storm 15, pleasure cruisers can go against the tide, as their speed under power means they can still make headway – less, precisely, the speed of tide they are battling. That night, the *Marchioness* left the Embankment near Trafalgar Square and headed east, downriver against the incoming tide. Aboard her was a happy cargo of partygoers, many of them recent graduates in their twenties ready for a night out of drinking and dancing in their happy little bright cocoon of a boat, the banks of the capital slowly slipping by through the night.

An hour or so earlier, a little further west, outside the cold, grey façade of the Nine Elms Cold Store, a building reputed to have played host to bloody cult rituals over the years, a small crew of men was mustering on the *Bowbelle*, also about to battle the tide to make passage downriver.

The *Bowbelle* had always been our most impressive river companion. At 262 ft long, her size and rough appearance had always fascinated us. She, and her sister ships of the time, the *Bowtrader* and *Bowsprit*, represented the dangerous romance of the dirty British coaster, a rough customer who'd been out to sea and to foreign shores, places that other, smaller, river-bound vessels could only dream of. You could hear her approach by the big-ship whine of her running gear. When she passed, she always elicited a respectful gaze and a few muttered comments. These were working giants in a world of toy boats, suction dredgers plying a trade sucking gravel off the Dutch shores and bringing it into London for use in construction. I wonder now how much of London is built of crushed Holland. At 1,475 tons unladen, the *Bowbelle* was a full ten times the size of the next-biggest craft west of the Thames Barrier and thirty-two times heavier than the *Marchioness*.

Our awe of the Bow fleet was only a romantic vision, a playful bit of anthropomorphism to while away long, occasionally dull days on the river, paddling our kayaks against a tide, or occasionally sailing, sat at the tillers of our little Topper and Laser dinghies, scrounging for a breath of wind between high buildings.

By 1.30 a.m. that night in 1989, the two vessels were making their way towards the sea. On one, a riot of youthful happiness, a birthday party, drinks and music. On the other, the hum of diesels, the crackle of Channel 14, the Port of London channel on VHF radio, and a small crew, most of them nursing hangovers from a bout of pretty serious daytime drinking. Soon, unbeknown to either, they were on a collision course, the faster *Bowbelle* creeping up behind the *Marchioness*, lit up like a fairground ride but invisible behind the big ship's gravel-dredging equipment. At 1.46 a.m., near Hungerford Bridge, the unthinkable happened and the *Bowbelle* struck the *Marchioness* obliquely, scraping down her flank, her great sea anchor ripping the pleasure boat's lid off as easily as a tin can.

Some of the 131 partygoers saw a huge black shadow loom above them. Some never knew what had hit them. Twenty-four drowned trapped below deck. One hundred and seven went into the water, some to be churned to pieces by the *Bowbelle*'s propellers. Eighty-six either swam to the banks or were picked up by the *Hurlingham*, the other party boat which had been following.

I remember my mother waking me with the news the next day. For someone to whom the Thames was a place of beaches, fun and sunshine, the news seemed hard to believe. And that disbelief was echoed in the press, whose initial reaction was one of incredulity that such an appalling disaster could have come, on a warm summer's night, in the middle of the capital – civilisation's safest cradle – with such little warning.

What few people know is that the accident was in many ways a repeat of what happened a century earlier on the Thames, a few miles further east in Woolwich – only, in that instance, more than 600 were killed, in the worst disaster on the Thames in recorded history. On 3 September 1878 the pleasure steamer *Princess Alice* was on a trip out of the city; a day out at the Kent Zoological and Botanical Gardens Institution, better known as Rosherville Gardens, at Gravesend, east of London in the estuary. These trips were popular at that time. By around 7.40 p.m., the 220-ft, 171-ton paddle steamer was on her way back into town, when she came across the much larger collier *Bywell Castle*, a 900-tonner on her way to pick up coal at Newcastle and sail it to Africa. A misunderstanding about each other's intended courses meant they collided in full view of each other. *Princess Alice* sunk in a few minutes, hundreds of passengers drowning below decks. Many of those who survived died later from the pollution they'd encountered in the river when fleeing the wreck. The drowned bodies became unnaturally bloated and required enlarged coffins for their interment. It seems there are as many ways to die on the water as there are craft that float upon its surface.

Not far from the scene of the *Marchioness* disaster, Lloyds of London keeps a large, black, hardbacked book, the latest in an inventory of hundreds. The records of ship losses from around the world are entered every day in the same quill pen that recorded clipper ship losses off Cape Horn in the nineteenth century. There is never a day when the quill is not dipped into its pot of ink.

Sixteen years after the *Marchioness* disaster, I was crossing the Channel on a small Thames river cruiser, 48 ft long, and built of mahogany planks on oak frames in 1935. It was a calm enough May day, but *Mimosa* was not made to go to sea and as her flat bottom repeatedly slapped the little waves, a few of us started swallowing and resolutely gazing at the horizon. Conversation faltered as the unmentionable malady stole over us: seasickness. I was with the *Mimosa*'s boatbuilder-owner Colin and his family and friends and we were en route from Ramsgate, on the Kentish coast, to France. Around us, a few dozen similar craft formed a motley fleet, but this was no ordinary pleasure trip. Every boat out there that day had taken part in Operation Dynamo in 1940, better known as the miraculous evacuation of British troops from the clutches of the advancing German army at Dunkirk, and it was to Dunkirk we were headed for a commemoration of that deliverance. Once tucked up in the little French harbour, something caught my eye – a familiar shape moored a few boats away. It was the *Hurlingham*, the *Marchioness*'s old playmate on the Thames, and built just eight years before her, in 1915, at the same yard – Salter Brothers in Oxford.

I recognised her immediately and wandered over to speak to her crew, burly characters whose main interests seemed to be lager and motorcycles. The *Hurlingham* saved lives at Dunkirk in the war, and picked up survivors from the sinking *Marchioness* nearly five decades later in 1989. Years later, I learned that the *Marchioness* had also survived Dunkirk before succumbing to the Thames in peacetime.

Today, the *Hurlingham* is still on the Thames and still available for party hire and later that day it crossed paths with us on its way downriver as we continued to head west. After sailing past the Houses of Parliament, these days protected by an exclusion zone that reaches out into the river, we reached the Westminster Boating Base, my old haunt and my stop for the night, marking the best day's distance run of the trip; a galactic 17 miles! I'd not been there for nearly twenty years, but two of the original staff were still there, including Adam, my early partner in canoeing crime, and Kevin, a keen historian of the Thames who knows the river like the back of his hand. I saw Julian to the pub and onto a tube, then had a quick but happy reunion with the Boating Base gang before I returned to pitch my tent on the club's pontoon. Kevin had warned the police in advance not to heed the sight of a small, lime-green tent pitched in the middle of the river not far from the Houses of Parliament and I slept like a stone, rocked to sleep by the wash of passing boats, the river of my youth rushing just a few feet below the wooden slats.

CHAPTER 21

THE RULES

Pimlico to Brentford on the River
Thames. Ten miles, thirteen
bridges. The rules of the road,
a new companion for the day, the
historic houseboats of the Thames
– and the Secret Air Service.

*If to starboard red do appear, 'tis
your duty to keep clear.*

Sailing school mnemonic

There are some who object to the arcane language of
sailing, believing that if the sea and the vessels that
float on it were accorded a landsman's dictionary (left and
right, forwards, backwards and so on), sailing would be
democratised for our anti-elitist age, stripped of its esoteric
aura for the benefit of great, fictional hordes of simple souls
who would love to go sailing – if only it didn't come with all
that tiresome baggage of history and magic.

Like most views of this sort, it is based on a dim view of the ability of others to absorb the same sort of complexity that the utterer of such statements has himself managed to achieve without too much strain. I've always found learning another language to be one of sailing's greatest appeals. Maritime English is a glossary born of utility: after all, there are so many parts of a boat and states of the sea, and they all needed a name. But it's also a beautiful, romantic language. A boat's structural ribs are called floors; so the floor of the cabin needs a different name: at sea, you walk not on a floor, but on a sole. Curve becomes sheer and a rope becomes a sheet. There are wonderfully ridiculous words too; to reduce the power of a four-sided mainsail you scandalise it – by deliberately deforming its shape, not by telling it a dirty joke. Furry, improvised socks twisted around ropes to stop them chafing are known as baggywrinkles. The sailors who talk about left and right rather than port and starboard, and going downstairs to use the loo rather than going below to use the heads, are missing out on a lot of fun: they're also playing their part in the erosion of meaning and history. I was determined that when my friend Dan showed up for the next leg back to Brentford in the western reaches of the Thames in London, he would learn the correct language for everything we did that day.

Once again, low water was early and by 6.30 a.m. I was pacing the pontoon, muttering sailing school mnemonics to myself and laughing out loud, all the while trying to find somewhere to pee, with high blocks of flats all around me.

This had been one of the biggest challenges of the trip, I reflected as I united water with water at a hidden edge, behind the sailing-dinghy cage. Dan was due in an hour's time, arriving on the Embankment above. Quite how I was going to collect him from the water, neither of us knew when we made our arrangement, but from here it was obvious, as an old solution to the problem appeared in the form of old stone steps, crumbling in places, and covered in dark green algae, leading down from the busy Grosvenor Road to the shingle beach below.

In its time, this little flight of steps would have been used by people wanting to cross the river before they went and built so many bridges. A waterman in a rowing boat would collect passengers from these steps and row them over to the other side. These days, it is kept from the river by a metal gate with iron spikes fringing the top. Dan appeared, climbing over the gate enthusiastically and ripping his shorts.

I started to drift towards him with the motor on idle, Dan jogging along the beach to keep up, the sun already hot, the river glittering and flat, and Battersea Power Station looming on my left. Just above, the Grosvenor Road was quiet behind its thick foliage of trees this early in the morning. I could just hear the odd taxi slowing down for traffic lights, maybe heading towards Heathrow Airport west of the city for an early morning flight. Dan waded as deep as his calves and hopped in, dripping in the warm water, and we were off. There wasn't enough wind to raise the sail, but suddenly, there seemed a lot to teach Dan. How to row, how to start an outboard motor... Then, with the tiny little outboard buzzing, we set off on our way. The headwinds were weak and fluky, not good enough to sail without having to tack all the way, and rowing could wait until later. Battersea Power Station rose above us, once the largest building in the world, and probably the subject of more grand designs by would-be saviours than any other building in London. One of the constants of growing up in London any time after 1983, when the coal-fired dinosaur stopped generating, was: what is the latest plan for Battersea Power Station? It actually comprises two identical power stations, one built in the 1930s, the second built in mirror image in the 1950s, providing the four-chimney silhouette familiar to anyone who's caught a train into London from the south – or anyone who bought the Pink Floyd album *Animals*. Today, its bricks were glowing, caught in the early morning sun.

The building is in a sorry state and it looks as though we will now be relying on yet another private developer turning it into yet more luxury flats, with sound systems plumbed throughout and no doubt a 'hand-made' kitchen – whatever is meant by that. Power stations use huge amounts of water for cooling, and I never tired of looking at the disused hulks of London's coal-fired past squatting by the sides of canals and rivers. Surbiton Power Station, which is now infested by tall grass and snakes; Battersea; Acton Lane on the Grand Union; and Bankside (now the Tate Modern). The most eerie of all is the monstrous edifice near Greenwich, with a white rendered exterior slowly peeling away over the years. Its ugly, block-like appearance somehow speaks of corrupted power and death. It's mired in rumours of dead bodies and witchcraft and it's not a place I'm keen to see the inside of.

After Battersea Bridge, Dan took the tiller for a while. River rule number one, applicable to all craft in any tideway: judge the power and direction of the current to see where it's pushing you. And there's one main reason for this: stationary objects in moving water. Dan was surprised at the power of the water pulling us past the moored houseboats, and residential boat moorings were coming thick and fast now as we left the centre of town behind for leafy west London. According to Chris Roberts in his zippy book *Cross River Traffic*, in the mid-nineteenth century a man called Thomas Barry was famous for sailing near here, plying a route between Vauxhall and Westminster Bridges in a 'tub' towed by four geese. I wonder if the geese ever learned the rules.

Here, armadas of houseboats in differing states of repair ride the tide, tethered – stilled forever as time and tide sweep up and down their flanks twice a day. Unlike the canals, the Thames can accommodate big boats, making this a much more interesting collection; *Bluebird of Chelsea*, a 52-ft river cruiser that once belonged to Malcolm Campbell, father of Donald who died on Coniston and even more of a speed freak, with nine land speed records and four water speed records to his name in the heady period between the two wars; ships and barges of all kinds, some wearing a rich, estuarine patina of rust over the protruding rivets holding their plates of steel or iron together. This is how little ships that used to ply the coastline end their days, converted for modern life with shore power, pot plants, bicycles on metal decks and high-speed wireless Internet. The accommodation is built down into old cargo holds and up over the sides of boats in large, boxy accommodation sheds. In the same way that all British high streets look the same until you look up and see the old buildings above, with their ornate window lintels and fading painted signs, all these boats look the same, unless you look down at their hull shapes. At Chelsea Moorings, one of these boxy superstructures towers above a sleek hull that once belonged to a World War Two high-speed launch, grey-painted wooden speedboats capable of 50 mph that would raid enemy shipping with torpedoes then run tail for home at full speed. These residential boats of the river are an unknown and undocumented patchwork of twentieth-century maritime history.

River rule number two: stick to the right-hand side of the river and if you need to cross, do so at right angles to your course, minimising the amount of time you are side-on to big river traffic which will be plying up and down fast in the deeper central channel – not that there was much traffic at that time in the morning.

River rule number three: if you don't know the lay of the land, always steer outside of moorings. If you go between moored boats and the bank, you'll meet the gangway that takes residents to their boats at some point. Depending on the height of these structures and the height of tide, you might not clear them, particularly if you have a mast. The consequences of that would be ugly and embarrassing at best, damaging and dangerous at worst.

Now we were approaching a building even more familiar to me than the silhouette of Battersea Power Station... Lots Road Power Station. I already knew it had ceased operation and was on its way to transformation into a block of flats. It didn't take much guesswork to figure that out. But it was a shock to see it, windows smashed, forgotten by the river it once sucked in and pumped out so greedily.

Back in the days when its cooling outlet was my playground, it wasn't just me and my immediate friends who used it. In 1991, we were to have some very special guests come to join us on the power station wave. That year, you couldn't go anywhere without hearing Bryan Adams singing 'Everything I Do' or someone saying 'I'll be back' in a gruff Austrian accent, after the release of *Terminator 2*. The First Gulf War was over, temporarily ending hostilities with the Middle East, and I'd just discovered the rap group Public Enemy. Life was good.

Ten years earlier, the SAS had stormed London's Iranian Embassy in a *Boy's Own* raid. The SAS were, and still are, a byword for manly heroism, with connotations of the warrior and espionage all rolled into one black-clad, high-tech universal soldier. Every boy – and no doubt every one of us – had an *SAS Survival Handbook* on our shelves at home. They are full of the most useful advice for the most unlikely situations. What to do when you drive into a lake; what to do in the aftermath of a nuclear explosion; how to build a shelter in the woods; how to use an ordinary biro to stab someone in the neck and give them an emergency tracheotomy. That one still makes me clutch my throat protectively every time I think of it. Little did we know that in the summer of 1991 we were about to meet the authors.

The director of the canoeing club pulled a few of us into his office one night after we came off the river. The club had received a request for a weekend of advanced instruction, including learning the rudimentary skills necessary to paddle on white water. Any break from helping novices paddle in a straight line or cajoling them into taking the dreaded spraydeck test (in which you capsize and remove the skirt that is worn around the waist and extends to the cockpit rim to keep water out) was welcome enough. When we found out who our willing pupils were, we could hardly contain ourselves. The bragging rights from this gig were going to be monumental. The Secret Air Service and Secret Boat Service were coming to our club.

For two days, we took six competent killers through the first steps to becoming competent white-water kayakers. With everyone else I'd taught it had taken months at best – usually years, to learn the first two basic manoeuvres: moving from a calm eddy into the fast flow (breaking in) and leaving that flow to catch the eddy on the other side (breaking out). It's not a complicated manoeuvre – if you lean downstream as you break in, you'll be fine. If you don't, you'll be flipped instantly. The difficulty in learning it is overcoming the powerful intuition to lean the wrong way. The SAS and SBS were the supermen we expected, but not in the way I thought they would be. Their power came not just from fearlessness, a quality they all possessed, but from an unexpected source that we had little respect for at the time: obedience. In putting their intuition aside and putting their trust in our instruction, they learned quickly and cheerfully. I've never before nor since had students as cheerful and strong. One of our jokes was their names: they all had generic names like Steve and Dave and John and it didn't take us long to twig that these weren't their real names.

We never charged the soldiers for their lessons, but a month later the favour was returned in a different way as we gathered outside the club at '0600 hours' on a clear autumn Saturday dawn. I was beginning to wonder if a practical joke had been played on us when a camouflaged military lorry pulled up and idled at the side of the road. In the secretive code of the elite forces, we weren't allowed to know where we were going, but we were off with our new friends to 'a forest in Kent' for a weekend. Pack warm clothes and survival bags, was all we'd been told.

After a couple of hours sat on wooden benches in the cloth-covered back of the lorry that billowed in the slipstream as we drove along the motorway, we reached our destination, stepping out into a glade in a thickly forested wood, with paths leading off to various metal huts and firing ranges. It was a relief to realise that we weren't about to stab each other in the throats with biros to perform emergency tracheotomies, and a disappointment to learn that we wouldn't be spending our short time setting off live grenades and blasting away at targets with AK-47s.

These days, with the likes of TV survivalists like Ray Mears and Bear Grylls spearheading the way, people pay good money to impale dead animal parts on the ends of sharpened sticks over fires – a murderous, meaty version of toasted marshmallows for adults. Back then it wasn't such a big thing. We were divided into three teams of four and given a chicken and a rabbit each as food for the night. For shelter, we were each given a standard bright-orange plastic bag to sleep in, and instructions on how to build a basic shelter. Immediately, problems became apparent. The first and most obvious was that our chicken was still alive. None of us in the group was a natural killer so our bird was despatched by one of the soldiers, who grasped its body in one hand, and pulled its neck sharply downwards with a twist using the other, making a sickening crunch as its neck broke. Gutting the beasts was fine – particularly a rabbit which you basically turn inside out, as the soldiers demonstrated. We sharpened twigs and tore the dead creatures apart, skewering disembodied bits on the end and toasting them in the fire as it grew dark, a surprisingly good feast with a sprinkle of salt. By the time we'd finished, the night was still young and all we had were two plastic bags and the embers of a fire. We hadn't bothered to build the shelter for the simple reason that we were lazy and stupid. By around 10 p.m. or so we were huddled, two in each plastic bag, squished uncomfortably close, shivering violently in our awkward intimacy.

Soon after that, two of our hosts arrived and half-dragged us to a huge bonfire, where our special forces friends were sat convivially, downing beers. Once we'd thawed out enough to be able to converse, we soon warmed to the task, getting slowly sozzled as we listened to stories through a long, cold October night. One man told us how he'd broken out of a military prison somewhere deep in the African continent using something like a toothbrush. Throughout the story, the man sat next to him kept nodding at us as though we thought the storyteller was lying. I can no longer remember where the jailbreak happened, and if I told you, they'd have to kill me.

We passed quickly into Putney on the spring flood and, with the wind behind us, put the sail up on a gentle run. London began to space out, growing greener as incredible mansions came down to the river's edge. It's a scene of rowers and willow trees, and, soon after Hammersmith, beautiful little wooded islands. Soon we were wondering whether we were still in London. We were in fact in boundary land, headed for Brentford Marina. When we arrived there, we tied the boat up to the floating pontoon outside. River rule number four: always approach stationary objects by travelling upstream, controlling your speed against the tide.

We went for a long walk down the canal and had a pub lunch and a few beers. When we left there, we threaded our way back through the endless, quiet suburban backstreets and silver-coloured people carriers of south-west London, and eventually found the tube. With nowhere to stay that night, I bade my farewell to Dan and returned home for the second time during the voyage.

I've mentioned that boat people are as bad as God people when it comes to evangelism, Dan being one of my early victims. Later that year, I got another friend wet on a kayak trip to the River Torridge in North Devon. George was working full-time as a teacher, had a full-time baby daughter and had just bought a house that needed full-time DIY. So he needed a break. We drove six hours west from the city on a cold November weekend, parking the car in a small lay-by. We dragged our boats behind us across a field, watched by the sheep who flocked together to stare, walking after us like in the parlour game, stopping every time we turned around. We slithered down the mudbank strapped into our boats and hit the river, taking off downstream.

Soon we were flowing down small rapids formed by reed beds growing in the middle of the river. For hours we saw no people and no sign that people had ever even existed. Our only companions in the water were a gold-and-green-patterned grass snake that swam across the river from one side to the other, and an otter that swam around us for a few moments, showing first his tail then his head. A heron, with its prehistoric, dinosaur shape, flew ahead of us and every time we caught him, took off and landed further downstream. A stork hid by the edge of the river and a bright kingfisher flitted from branch to branch. With the reed banks separating the water into braided channels, the large wading birds and unidentified birds of prey circling overhead, the sun appearing out of season to burn off the cloud cover that had been there in the morning, we might have been on a little tributary of the Nile in Uganda. The canoe has the least impact of any watercraft and the creatures who shared the river with us seemed barely to heed our passing. We tried to be as quiet as them, slicing our paddles smoothly and quietly through the water. On we went, mile after mile, the river accelerating in the braided channels through reeds into ruffles and white peaks and we floated down them, riding them around the edge of the river and ducking under the tree branches, extracting every cubic metre of hydraulic power the river gave us.

Later, we saw two wires across the river and a man in a tiny home-made cage strung between them pulling himself across. We hailed him three times before he finally responded, not delighted to see us, maybe embarrassed to be caught in such an eccentric, private act. Later, we passed a fly-fisherman out to the top of his waders enjoying some illicit fishing after the end of the season. We stayed the night in a man's back garden, next to a children's climbing frame and slide. The next morning we arose early to struggle into wet, muddy gear and ride the rest of the river down to the sea. We were cold and, thanks to a night on the tiles of the local town the night before, hung-over as hell. I'm not sure we were having that much fun 25 miles later as we hauled ourselves and our boats up the steep, muddy bank of the little town of Bideford – but in memory it was a magical trip. Happiness is sometimes better remembered than experienced.

CHAPTER 22

TRAMPING

Brentford to Surbiton on the Thames
and Upper Thames. Eight miles,
nine bridges and three locks.

*When you have completed 95 per cent of
the journey, you are only halfway there.*

JAPANESE MAXIM

My cousin Ben joined me at Brentford the next morning for the final run back to Surbiton. Ben enjoys all sorts of tortuous cardio challenges that involve cycling, swimming and running, and that was fine by me – he could row. He also enjoys climbing mountains, something that requires a good strength-to-body-mass ratio and a head for heights. I have neither, but we took turns at the oars, sending the boat through the water at a good lick, and later raised the sails for a while when we got a breeze.

Just outside the shelter of Brentford Marina in the Thames, we rowed past a little wooded island called Lot's Ait. Ait means, in the language of the Thames, 'island'. This one has three large building sheds dipping down to the waterline, dilapidated, rusting and forgotten.

This was where they used to build the lighters that are, as I have already said, such a common sight in central London at anchor – unpowered metal barges of 80 ft and as many tons that would be rowed by the lightermen who would work their huge oars standing up. These days, they are filled with the city's rubbish and towed by tug to the estuary, but for years, they would unload cargoes from ships in the Port of London and bring them upriver to here, where they could join the canal network. The boatyard on Lot's Ait was established in the 1920s but its trade was attacked in the 1950s and 1960s from a number of angles, most importantly, the containerisation of seagoing cargo and the coming of the motorways to London. The owners of the yard never even liquidated their assets. In 1970, they just put their tools down and left, walking away from an era and off the island, crossing its little bridge to the main riverbank for the last time. Old bits of machinery nestled, rusting, in overgrown grass and a couple of barges sat outside on the low tide, unmolested for four decades.

Soon the island will reopen for business, this time catering for DIY boatbuilders and restorers, men who will keep little boats there and potter around the yard on Sunday afternoons covered in splashes of paint and varnish, west London's answer to the Greenwich Yacht Club. Often, restoring an old wooden boat to as-new condition involves a total rebuild and represents a lot more work than starting the job from scratch. Plank after plank is found to be rotten and, by the time the boat is finished, little or none of the original remains. This raises an interesting, and ancient, philosophical question: Theseus's Paradox. It has exercised Heraclitus, Socrates, Plato, Plutarch, Hobbes and Locke, and it goes, in modern terms, something like this:

A man falls in love with an old 1930s sailing yacht down on her luck, sitting in a field somewhere with weeds growing through the planks. He puts it on a low-loader, drives it to a boatyard and asks the boatbuilder to restore the apple of his eye to her original glory. The boatbuilder starts by replacing the leaky old deck, discovers the mast is rotten too, so he makes another to the same template in similar timber – 'replacing like with like' in the solid jargon of the boatbuilder. He has new sails cut. Then he starts on the planking of the hull, removing and replacing one at a time. All the while, he is tossing bits of the old boat onto a pile nearby. Another boatbuilder takes a look at the pile of old wood and decides the first man was a bit hasty; the wood's not that bad after all. So he starts using it to build a second version to exactly the same design. Eventually, both boats are complete and looking great, all new paint, varnished wood and gleaming bronze. Our customer returns to collect his boat and when he arrives, he hears the story of the two yachts. The question then is: which one is his boat? Or to put it a different way, does a thing's identity live in its design and purpose or in its physical substance? If you want a very long conversation with a man restoring a boat, I recommend you tell him the story of Theseus's Ship. The answer lies within our own bodies, which nearly entirely regenerate every decade or so. Very little of you or me is 'original' so clearly identity lies in design rather than substance. So it was with wooden ships, which were also refitted regularly, each time losing original fabric, constantly regenerating themselves to withstand the rigours of the seas they must sail on.

Our timing with the tides was accidentally just right and we free-flowed through where the weir at Richmond would have been on a flowing tide, avoiding the need to lock through. Later that day, when we tied up at Teddington Locks, the lock-keeper came out and asked: 'Did you know that the famous fish-slap dance from *Monty Python* was filmed here?'

Not long after that, we tied up outside the Thames Sailing Club and I stepped off the little Storm 15 for the last time and had a long look at the boat. The dark green paintwork was scarred deeply on both flanks, and the decks were dyed in a patina of river mud and grain of sand. And I still hadn't told her builders about the broken rowlock...

Later that evening, some of the Thames Sailing Club members threw a little celebration party for my effort and we sat out on the balcony, one of the few places in

London you can be by the river and watch the sun sink all the way down to the horizon. Nobody thought to ask me the unanswerable question that evening: why? They all knew why someone would want to sail around London in a continuous loop. But, later, as more people asked, I was forced to think about it.

On one level, the reasons were simple: I like journeying in small boats, being outdoors and walking in the city. Sailing and rowing around London was like a better version of a long city walk – better because there was no walking involved, but with the same sense of internal space moving through a slow kaleidoscope. I realised much later that I was also trying to make sense of the place I call home, trying to immerse myself in my own context. Ten days drinking fine whisky in the sun with a bit of sailing thrown in is hardly a voyage of self-discovery, but I did learn a lot about the city – mostly how large it is.

Every journey in London, whether by boat, on foot, by car, bike, bus, tube or train, is a single strand in a great heap of spaghetti, one of an infinite number of journeys to an infinite number of destinations that grows as the city expands ever outwards. The city is like a game of consequences in this respect: Christopher Wren draws churches and cathedrals, and makes an attempt to design the entire city, but that chance is denied him, so he folds his bit of paper over and hands it on. Joseph Bazalgette sucks his pencil for a while, then draws a sewer system and a great stone embankment running down the side of the Thames to contain it. The river grows faster and narrower and more wavy. In more recent years, the Docklands become part of the modern, service-industry city of the eighties, then the London Docklands Development Company hands the sheet on, and it keeps getting folded and, eccentrically, the conurbation grows. Whole areas die and disappear as new ones come into being on the fringes of the city. The Thames Estuary will be next, with thousands of new homes planned, as well as the possibility of the island airport. It will even have a new name – the optimistic politico's slogan of 'Gateway'.

You don't have to sail and row around London to feel its immensity. A look at a tube map will do that. There are places in London I don't know well – like Wembley, Putney and Finchley. There are others I've heard of but never visited, like Plaistow and Brockley. Strangest of all, there are entire districts that I've never even heard of. It seems hardly a week goes by without mention of a far-off star in the galaxy of the metropolis. Keston, for instance, or places like Dollis Hill, as strange as the moon, still leap out from the pages of maps to remind me how little I know of the place I call home. I see them on the tube map and wonder who would want to live there. What is life like there? What do they do? Why don't they live where I live?

Seeing new parts of the place I call home was one of the reasons I went. Another reason was the opposite: I thought that by binding it with a single string, a perfect journey, going from A to A and with almost no repetition, I could control it; rationalise the city and mark its outer territory, the same way a cat or dog will mark the outer limit of its garden. On the many days I didn't pass a loo, the similarity was even more striking.

In the end, though, it was the other way round: it was the waters of the old city that controlled me, making me once again a victim to the whims of the city. Their routes predetermined, they change for no one, and the views of the splendour and back doors of the city change but slowly. I went to see the city, but in the end it was the canals and the rivers that became the focus of the journey. Of all people, I should have guessed that might happen.

That night, the weather finally broke; aside from one lovely week in May, Britain never did get the fine summer it was promised by the forecasters that year.

I drove home in a light, warm rain and immediately emailed Matt Newland, owner of one very damaged dinghy, to warn him of the state of his boat before he laid his eyes on it when I delivered it back to him. The next day, there was a six-word reply waiting for me: 'Don't worry,' he wrote, 'boats are for using.'

ACKNOWLEDGEMENTS

To the people who either made the trip more possible, more enjoyable or more affordable: Matt and Nick Newland; Ben May and all who contributed to Sail 4 Cancer; Thames Sailing Club; Peter Willis; Chris Symonds at Brentford Marina; Brian at Brentford Lock; Jeremy Batch at Limehouse Lock; all at the CA at Limehouse; Kevin Burke and Adam White at WBB; the London Canal Museum; Darryl Taylor, Louise Busby, Julian Harrap, Dan Mackie, Ben Atherton, my sister and immediate family, Frank the hermit – and anyone I've been messing about on the water with for the last twenty-five years, particularly sailors and canoeists, who are the best company of all. I owe a special debt of gratitude to Miles Kendall for his help in seeing this book make it to print and, most of all, to my publishers Claire Plimmer, Abigail Headon and all at Summersdale for days of sympathetic, accurate work in making that happen, among them Robert Smith for his inspired front cover and map and Ray Hamilton for spotting my many errors and repetitions.

NARROWBOAT
DREAMS

*A Journey
North by
Englands
Waterways*

**STEVE
HAYWOOD**

NARROWBOAT DREAMS

A Journey North by England's Waterways

Steve Haywood

ISBN: 978-1-84024-670-4   Paperback   £8.99

Steve Haywood has a problem. He doesn't know where he comes from. In the south, people think he's a northerner; in the north, they think he's from the south. Judged against global warming and the sad demise of *Celebrity Big Brother*, this hardly registers highly on the Richter scale of world disasters. But it's enough to worry Steve. And it's enough of an excuse for him to escape the routine of his life in London for a voyage of discovery along England's inland waterways.

Travelling by traditional narrowboat, he heads north from Banbury in deepest Oxfordshire, through the former industrial wastelands of the the now vibrantly modern Manchester, to the trendy affluence of Hebden Bridge at the centre of West Yorkshire's ciabatta belt. With irrepressible humour he describes the history of the canals, his encounters with characters along the way, and the magic that makes England's waterways so appealing.

'Haywood imprints his inimitable humour on his descriptions of the people and places he meets along the way.'
BBC COUNTRY FILE magazine

'... an enjoyable, moreish read, and one of the better British canal travelogues of recent years'   WATERWAYS WORLD

'With irrepressible humour, he describes the history of the canals, his encounters with characters along the way and the magic that makes England's waterways so appealing.'   BEST OF BRITISH

Have you enjoyed this book?
If so, why not write a review on your favourite website?

If you're interested in finding out more about our travel books, friend us on Facebook at **Summersdale Traveleditor** and follow us on Twitter: **@SummersdaleGO**

Thanks very much for buying this Summersdale book.

www.summersdale.com